Baseball's Great Dynasties
THE
Mets

Baseball's
Great Dynasties
THE
Mets

Bill Gutman

GALLERY BOOKS
An imprint of W.H. Smith Publishers Inc.
112 Madison Avenue
New York, New York 10016

Published by Gallery Books
A Division of W.H. Smith Publishers Inc.
112 Madison Avenue
New York, New York 10016

Produced by
Brompton Books Corp.
15 Sherwood Place
Greenwich, CT 06830

ISBN 0-8317-0628-7

Printed in Hong Kong

10 9 8 7 6 5 4 3 2 1

PICTURE CREDITS

All photos courtesy of UPI/Bettmann Newsphotos except the following:
Courtesy, Glenn Peterson: 34(top).
  Ponzini Photography: 2, 3, 7, 52, 54(top, center),
  55(all three), 56, 57(all four), 58, 59(center, bottom), 60, 61(top, bottom), 63(right), 64(bottom left),
  66, 69(top, center), 71, 72, 73, 74, 75, endsheets.
  Bruce Schwartzman: 62(top), 63(left), 64(bottom
  right), 65, 67(top, bottom), 69(bottom), 70, 76, 77.

ACKNOWLEDGMENTS

The author and publisher would like to thank the following people who helped in the preparation of this
book: Don Longabucco, the designer; Susan Bern-
stein, the editor; Rita Longabucco, the picture editor;
and Elizabeth McCarthy, the indexer.

Page 1: *Tim Teufel, Howard Johnson, Bob Ojeda, and Ron Darling don the latest variation of the rally cap during the 1986 season.*

Page 2: *In 1986 Gary Carter tied the then team record for runs batted in – set by Rusty Staub 10 years earlier – with 105 ribbies.*

Page 3: *Keith Hernandez, a 6-time Gold Glove winner as a Met, was the defensive leader on the field for the club.*

This page: *Legendary Willie Mays is greeted at the dugout after hitting what would prove to be his last major league home run – number 660.*

Contents

Preface

For many baseball fans in New York City, the end of the 1957 baseball season also meant the end of their diamond world as they knew it. The persistent rumors that the Big Apple might be losing one or two of its three teams had suddenly become a reality.

It was the New York Giants who announced first. The Jints had been a National League staple in New York since 1883. But on August 19, 1957, the team ownership said it would be moving the ball club to San Francisco, California, a coast away. Then on October 8, the Brooklyn Dodgers confirmed what everyone already knew. They, too, would be going to the West Coast, to the glitz and glamor that was Los Angeles. So when the 1958 season opened, only the New York Yankees would be left for the many baseball fans of the city to see.

But for baseball hungry New Yorkers, the rather large presence that was the Bronx Bombers simply wasn't enough. For as good as the Yankees were, the Dodgers and Giants had both loyal followings and long traditions. And both ball clubs had been fiercely competitive during the 1950s. In fact, when they faced each other the result was often tantamount to war.

Now they were leaving. Not surprisingly, the question of how the void would be filled was quickly raised. For decades, except for an occasional franchise shift, baseball had remained the same – eight teams in the National League, eight in the American. So how could New York hope for a team to replace the departed Giants and Dodgers? Could they lure an existing team to the city? If that happened, the new club would either have to share Yankee Stadium or

Below: *Davey Johnson (5) was the most successful manager in Mets annals. He was the New York skipper from 1984 to early 1990.*

Opposite: *Outfielder Mookie Wilson (1) gets high fives from happy teammates during the winning years in the 1980s.*

Right: *Pitcher Tom Seaver as he tried a brief comeback in 1987. As a rookie 20 years earlier, Seaver won 16 games and was the Mets first superstar.*

Opposite top: *The main reasons for the Mets title team in 1986. Left to right, Darryl Strawberry, Keith Hernandez, Dwight Gooden, Gary Carter and Manager Dave Johnson.*

Opposite bottom: *Former Brooklyn Dodger stars Gil Hodges (l) and Duke Snider (c) join the Mets first ever manager, Casey Stengel, at the start of the 1963 season.*

play at the Polo Grounds. Neither prospect seemed bright.

Then at the outset of the 1960s baseball began to change. The success of the Dodgers and Giants on the West Coast proved once and for all that the national pastime could truly be national. The lords of the game decided that the time was right to expand.

It started with the American League. In 1961, two new teams were added. The Los Angeles Angels (later to be known as the California Angels) became the first American League team on the West Coast and a new Washington Senators team was also added to the league. The old Senators franchise had moved to Minnesota and become the Twins.

The league also went to a 162-game schedule to accommodate the new teams. With phase one of the expansion completed, it was now time for the second stage. And this was the one New York fans were anticipating. Beginning with the 1962 season, National League baseball would be returning to the Big Apple with the New York Mets.

1. The Early Years—Casey at the Helm

The Mets (symbolizing the New York *metropolitan* area), for want of a better home, would be playing in the old Polo Grounds, the former home of the New York Giants. If nothing else, there were a ton of baseball memories contained there. The second new franchise for 1962 was located in Houston, Texas, where the club would be called the Colt 45's (later called the Astros).

Of course, as with any new team the first task would be to choose a manager and then players. The choice of manager was easy, almost a natural, and really a coup for the new team. He was Charles Dillon "Casey" Stengel, a beloved figure in New York base-

ball circles and for good reason. Ol' Case or the "Old Professor," as he was called, had been the highly successful manager of the New York Yankees from 1949 to 1960. During that time, Stengel piloted the Bombers to 10 American League pennants and 7 World Series triumphs.

But after the Yanks lost the 1960 Series to the Pittsburgh Pirates in seven games, Casey was unceremoniously fired. Too old, was the implication. Now, after being out of baseball for just one year, the old skipper was back. Stengel would be 72 years old at the outset of the 1962 season, but he still knew the game, knew talent, and had that wonderful, engaging personality. No matter how bad the team might be on the field, Ol' Case would be an asset and an attraction. He liked nothing better than to entertain the press and media with his baseball stories, told in a unique kind of language someone had fittingly dubbed "Stengelese."

As for getting players, that was another thing. Each existing team could only protect so many players on their 40-man rosters. The others would be available for the new teams to draft. Both the Mets and Colt 45's would be allowed to draft 20 players. They could, of course, sign other veterans who had been cut loose as well as untried youngsters looking for a place to play. Like any expansion team, the Mets would have a mixture of veterans, youngsters, and journeymen, with few or no real top-notch performers.

There were, however, a few bright spots on that first Mets ball club. Veteran outfielders Frank Thomas and Richie Ashburn both came with credible backgrounds. Infielders Charlie Neal and Felix Mantilla were also considered solid, while longtime Yankee outfielder Gene Woodling added yet another reliable bat. Right-hander Roger Craig and lefty Al Jackson were the best of the makeshift pitching staff.

The team also signed a former Brooklyn Dodger, a man who was already a legend in New York. He was Gil Hodges, the power-hitting first baseman of the Dodger teams of the late 1940s and 1950s. But Hodges was 38 years old in 1962, reduced to part-time

status. Though he managed to hit nine homers, he was a shell of his former self and would make his mark on the team in a distinctly different way a few short years later.

But trying to put together elements of a team to please the fans and win definitely wasn't easy. While a few of the aforementioned players were capable of contributing to established, solid teams, playing for an expansion ball club was another story. The nearly one million fans who came out to the Polo Grounds to see the new team in 1962, quickly found that out. The first edition of the Mets was not only bad, it was horrid. They were, by far, the worst of the four expansion teams that joined the majors in 1961 and 1962.

The pitching ranged from erratic to downright awful. The fielding was shoddy, mental errors often leading to physical miscues and the hitting, though somewhat better, wasn't enough to compensate for the rest. The 1962 Mets set a major league record for futility by winning just 40 games while losing 120. The Colt 45's, by contrast, finished at 64-96, nothing to write home about, but still 24 games better than the Mets in the standings. In fact, the Houston team finished in eighth place, also beating out the Chicago Cubs.

Not surprisingly, the Mets lost their first game ever, 11-4, to the St. Louis Cardinals and it was downhill from there. In fact, the club lost their first nine contests and for a while it looked as if they would never win one. Finally, a young right-hander named Jay Hook went the distance to beat the Pirates, 9-1, at Forbes Field, giving the Mets their first win in franchise history.

But before the season ended, the new club from New York had become a laughing-stock, a new measure of ineptitude, a study in futility that only the wonderful humor of Casey Stengel could somewhat offset.

It was Ol' Case who first referred to the

Above: *The first Mets team in 1962 was composed of over-the-hill vets, untried youngsters and mediocre journeyman players.*

Below left: *Gil Hodges (r) chats with Hall of Famer Rogers Hornsby, who was a Mets batting coach in 1962.*

Below right: *Veteran Richie Ashburn was one of the few bright spots on the 1962 Mets. The fleet center-fielder hit .306 with the Amazins, then retired.*

Top: *The hard-luck starters of the 1962 Mets. (l to r) Roger Craig, Jay Hook, Bob Miller, Craig Anderson, and Al Jackson.*

Above: *Veteran lefty "Vinegar Bend" Mizell (l) and first sacker Marv Throneberry (c) are chatting with coach "Cookie" Lavagetto, a former Brooklyn Dodger hero.*

team as "my Amazins." But the venerable skipper, like everyone else, was really amazed at what the club couldn't do and the number of ways they could find to lose ball games.

Total futility might have been the best way to describe that first Mets team. Roger Craig and Al Jackson, the team's two best pitchers, kept finding new ways to lose. They would finish the year at 10-24 and 8-20 respectively. Young Jay Hook, who had a propensity for putting a stop to losing streaks, wound up at 8-19. A journeyman right-hander named Craig Anderson, lost 16 in a row and finished at 3-17, while the team's first ever draft choice Bob Miller was

1-12. And if that doesn't add up to big league losing, nothing does.

Thomas had a fine year with 34 homers and 94 ribbies, while veteran Ashburn hit .306 in 389 at bats. But seeing the kind of team he was now with, the cagey center-fielder decided to retire a .300 hitter and move into the broadcast booth. First base-man Marv Throneberry, despite becoming a symbol of the team's ineptitude, belted 16 homers, Jim Hickman had 13 and Charlie Neal managed 11 with 58 RBIs.

But more than once as that first, long season dragged to its 120-loss conclusion, manager Stengel was known to throw his hands in the air and lament:

"Can't anyone here play this game?"

There were losing streaks of 17 games, 13 games, and 11 games. The first excitement during that first season came when the Giants and Dodgers returned to town to play the Mets. The fans filled the old ball-park to scream deliriously for Willie Mays, who would lead his Giants to a pennant in a great race with the Dodgers. The L.A. team still had a few of the old Brooklyn heroes, like Duke Snider, Johnny Podres, Don Drysdale, and Sandy Koufax.

Finally, and maybe mercifully, the season was over and the most anyone could say was that at least National League baseball had returned to New York. Plans were afoot for a brand new stadium in the borough of Queens, but the club would still have to play one more year in the ancient

Polo Grounds. And as 1963 approached, it was difficult to see the team getting any better. A few of the players had changed, but the script looked to be pretty much the same.

Basically, it was. But there were a few new individuals who helped bring the fans out to the tune of just over one million. First there was Duke Snider. The great Duke of Flatbush returned to New York, close to the scene of his starring years with the Dodgers. Though in the twilight of a Hall of Fame career, the Duke still managed 14 homers and 45 RBIs to give old Brooklyn fans a taste of nostalgia and new Mets fans a few thrills.

There were, however, a couple of other positive additions. Rookie second baseman Ron Hunt proved to be a real find, a hustling, scrapping kind of player who wasn't afraid to put his body on the line to win a ball game. Hunt would bat a solid .272 and finish second in the Rookie of the Year balloting to a similar type second baseman on the Cincinnati Reds who did things just a little bit better. His name was Pete Rose.

In addition, the club unveiled an 18-year-old first baseman, a homegrown product from New York, named Ed Kranepool. Kranepool had a three-game stint as a 17-year-old the season before, but in 1963 would play in 86 games and bat .209. It was the beginning of a Mets career that would last through 1979 and see some significant contributions.

Otherwise, there wasn't much help. Gil Hodges played 11 games, then went off to manage the Washington Senators. Frank

Thomas saw his power numbers down to 15 homers and 60 RBIs. He was on the downside. Craig set a club record with an 18-game losing streak and wound up with a record of 5-22. Al Jackson did better at 13-17, while Carlton Willey, who had come over from the Braves, was a 9-14 pitcher. It all added up to a 51-111 finish, just a little better than 1962.

The club was still dead last, of course, finishing an embarrassing 15 games behind their expansion counterpart, the Colt 45's, and 48 games out of first place.

Above: *Manager Casey Stengel and outfielder Duke Snider check out the ancient Polo Grounds, where the Mets played their first two years. The Polo Grounds had been the NY Giants' home until they moved to San Francisco in 1958.*

Left: *The early Mets did some things right. Here first baseman Tim Harkness awaits the throw that nailed Cincinnati superstar Frank Robinson by several strides during a Mets 4-1 victory in 1963.*

2. Moving on to the Big Shea

The 1964 season was a significant one for New York baseball. In the Bronx, the Yankees were completing another run of five consecutive American League pennants. But little did anyone know at the outset of the season that 1964 would mark a significant change in Yankee fortunes. It would, in effect, be a last hurrah for the proud Bronx Bombers. Beginning the following year the team would go into an eclipse, not winning another AL flag for a dozen years. And this would open the town up for the fledgling Mets.

That same year, 1964, the Mets took the first real step toward respectability and stability by moving into their brand new home in Queens. Shea Stadium was located right next to the huge World's Fair which was already attracting hordes of people and was positioned to pull in fans from all over the five boroughs of New York City. The big ballpark could hold more than 55,000 fans. Now all the team had to do was become competitive.

It was hard to see that happening in 1964. The ball club was still not producing its own young talent. Besides building an expansion team, it also takes time to build a minor league organization to nurture and develop young players. So the third edition of the Mets had basically the same mixture of marginal talent that had characterized the first two losing teams. And the result was the same.

The team would lose 109 games in 1964, an improvement of only two games over the 1963 ball club. Ol' Case was still at the helm, lamenting and entertaining at the same time, but some people were getting restless. Even though 1,732,597 fans passed through the Shea Stadium turnstiles during the Mets first season there, many felt it was time the team began to build toward a winner. There was very little visible progress.

Only second baseman Ron Hunt stood out. In his second full season, Hunt batted .303 and more importantly became the first

Below: *The formal dedication of Shea Stadium took place in April of 1964. Workmen were rushing to complete the outfield wall even as the ceremony took place. The Mets new home was built at a cost of $25 million.*

Far left: *Manager Stengel welcomes two great vets to the team in 1965. They are pitcher Warren Spahn (l) and catcher Yogi Berra. Both players, as well as Ol' Case, would wind up in Baseball's Hall of Fame.*

Left: *The Mets thought they finally had a home-grown slugger when rookie Ron Swoboda belted 19 home runs in 1965.*

Below: *It was a happy 76th birthday for Casey Stengel in July of 1966. Ol' Case had retired after breaking a hip a year earlier. But he returned to Shea for the celebration and to pilot a team of old-timers in a re-creation of the 1950 All-Star Game.*

Met player ever to be voted a starting berth on the National League All-Star team. That, in itself, was quite an honor.

At first glance, 1965 was little more than business as usual for the Mets. On April 12, the club lost its opening day game for the fourth straight year. And when the season ended, the Amazins were in last place for the fourth consecutive time. What's more, their 50-112 record represented absolutely no improvement over the previous two years. In fact, the final mark was the team's worst since their first season of 1962.

But the bottom line notwithstanding, the 1965 season was a significant one for the ball club in a number of ways. A slow and almost subtle changing of the guard was beginning to take place at every level of the team.

While two great veteran players, catcher Yogi Berra and pitcher Warren Spahn joined the ball club for a last hurrah, there were also some interesting youngsters on board. Ron Swoboda was a 20-year-old outfielder from Baltimore who made the starting lineup, and by the end of April was leading the majors in homers. Though he would tail off and wind up with just 19 for the year, many felt the team had found a slugger of its own.

Pitcher Tug McGraw was a hard-throwing left-hander from California. Like Swoboda, he was just 20 years old at the start of the 1965 campaign and the club swung him back and forth between the bullpen and starting assignments. Tug was just 2-7 for the year, though he had a respectable, 3.32 earned run average.

The biggest event of 1965, however, also proved to be the saddest. On July 24, just six days before his 75th birthday, manager Stengel took a fall resulting in a broken hip. At his age, Ol' Case couldn't run the

ball club in that conditon and was replaced by coach Wes Westrum, who had been a catcher with the New York Giants in the early 1950s. Though he would live another 10 years, Casey Stengel would never manage again. It was a big loss for baseball. There would never be another like the Old Professor.

Under Westrum, the Mets staggered home to still another last place finish. Kranepool led the team in hitting with only a .253 average. Swoboda had 19 home runs to pace the club in that department, while third sacker Charlie Smith had 62 RBIs. There was very little real offense so the pitchers suffered.

Jack Fisher finished at 8-24, while Al Jackson was 8-20. Both had pitching talent. It was hard to see any improvement despite the nominal changes. To most fans, there

Right: *Wes Westrum was the new Mets manager after Ol' Case left. But the former Giants' catcher didn't look happy when he resigned from the job in September of 1967.*

Below right: *Righthander Tom Seaver was the Mets' first Rookie of the Year in 1967. Two years later he became the team's first Cy Young Award winner with a 25-7 record as the club won the world's championship.*

didn't seem to be any plan, any real blueprint for winning. Yet the fans continued to push through the Shea Stadium turnstiles. There were another 1.7 million in 1965 and then in 1966 attendance came close to reaching 2 million.

Maybe that's because the team finally fought its way out of the National League basement. And for the Mets, that was almost tantamount to winning the pennant.

It wasn't that the 1966 Mets were world beaters. By no means. But the ball club was good enough to win 66 games, the best record by far in their short history. And their 66-95 record under Wes Westrum enabled the club to finish 7½ games ahead of the last place Cubs and just 5½ behind the eighth place Houston Astros (the team name had been changed from Colt 45's).

Another pair of young players joined the team in 1966, both of whom would make their presence known in upcoming years. They were leftfielder Cleon Jones and catcher Jerry Grote. Ron Hunt had rebounded from injuries to lead the club with a .288 average, while Ed Kranepool blasted 16 home runs and veteran third baseman Ken Boyer, acquired from St. Louis, drove home a team-leading 61 runs.

Jack Fisher, Dennis Ribant, and Bob Shaw all won 11 games, Ribant and Shaw at 11-9 and 11-10 respectively, posting winning records. Four players drove in 50 or more runs. But there was still no superstar, no pitching leader, no one player who would lead the way out of the abyss. Then, a year later, that player arrived and the face of the

New York Mets would be changed forever.

His name was George Thomas Seaver, called Tom by his teammates. Later he would become known as Tom Terrific or simply "The Franchise." But in 1967, he was a 22-year-old rookie out of the University of Southern California.

After signing with the Mets, Seaver pitched one year in the minors where he compiled a 12-12 record. But he was better than that, much better. In fact, he was called by one writer a 21-year-old player with a 35-year-old head, a compliment to his pitching prowess.

When the Mets looked at that same prowess in the spring of 1967, then looked at the rest of their staff, they decided to keep Seaver in the big leagues. It proved a wise move for everyone. For despite the fact that the Mets were not a very good baseball team in 1967, Tom Seaver gave the club another dimension. He was a winner, a guy who made it clear that he didn't like to lose.

With Seaver on the mound, the Mets were competitive. Without him, they were the same old doormats, back in the basement and not looking very good. The team returned to the cellar with a 61-101 record. It was so disappointing that manager West-

rum resigned just before the season ended. Coach Salty Parker directed the team through its final 11 games.

But a look beyond the dismal record showed something else. And it began with Tom Seaver. Tom was the Mets only winning pitcher, posting a 16-13 record for the year. His numbers indicate that his record would have been even better had he been pitching for a contender. He had 18 complete games in 34 starts, posted an impressive 2.76 earned run average, threw a pair of shutouts and fanned 170 hitters while walking just 78. It was obvious that he was no ordinary rookie and he soon became the first Met ever to win a post-season award when he was named National League Rookie of the Year.

On the surface, there wasn't much else to cheer about. However, the young players continued to appear in the lineup. Kranepool, Swoboda, and Cleon Jones all still showed potential. Grote was a fine catcher, and now they were joined by shortstop Bud Harrelson. He would give the club a solid, professional shortstop for years to come. Veteran Ed Charles became the latest in a long line of candidates to take over at third.

But aside from Seaver, the pitching was still weak. However, the ball club was in the process of doing something about it. After six years, the minor league organization was beginning to nurture and produce quality players. Then, shortly after the 1967 season ended, the team made what was perhaps the most important move of all.

On October 11, Gil Hodges was named as the new Mets' manager. The former Brooklyn Dodger star was a leader who, at 43, had learned his craft well. After retiring as a player early in 1963, Hodges took over the helm of the Washington Senators. Though working with an expansion team with few top players, he had the club improving each year. He was the man the Mets wanted and as it turned out, the man they needed.

As a manager, Gil Hodges was the strong, silent type, who was always straight with his players. The new skipper would team with new general manager Johnny Murphy to begin overhauling the

Below: *Shortstop Bud Harrelson was the glue that held the Mets infield together in the late 1960s and early 1970s. The wily Harrelson would later become a coach and then the team's manager in 1990.*

Right: *When former Brooklyn Dodger star Gil Hodges became the Mets manager in 1968, the team's fortunes began to change. Hodges turned the club from a perennial loser to world champs in just two years.*

Above: *Nolan Ryan joined the Mets as a hard-throwing 21-year-old rookie in 1968. No one knew then that they were seeing baseball's future strikeout king. Nolan never really found his niche with the Mets and had to achieve stardom elsewhere.*

tial star, a strikeout pitcher with a tremendous fastball. Only his inability to find the plate often enough made him a question mark. Veterans Don Cardwell, Cal Koonce, Ron Taylor, and the returning Al Jackson added stability.

A trade with the Chicago White Sox brought centerfielder Tommie Agee to the team. Agee would join Cleon Jones and Ron Swoboda to give the club a young and exciting outfield. Veteran Art Shamsky was acquired to back them up. Veterans Phil Linz and Al Weis were on hand to back up youngsters Harrelson and second baseman Ken Boswell and another vet, J.C. Martin, came in to spell Grote behind the plate.

Though they weren't pennant contenders, the 1968 Mets were no longer pushovers. In fact, with Seaver and Koosman on the mound, the Mets could be as tough as any team in the league. With just a little more pitching and a little more hitting . . . well, maybe their fans were dreaming.

As it turned out, the team finished ninth in its first year with Gil Hodges at the helm. But the 73-89 record was the best in the team's history. And there were definitely bright spots.

Koosman was as good as everyone hoped, posting a 19-12 record. Throwing 264 innings, the lefty from Appleton, Minnesota, completed 17 of 34 starts, tossed an impressive 7 shutouts, fanned 178 hitters and had an earned run average of just 2.08. It was hard to ask for anything more.

Seaver followed his fine rookie year with a 16-12 effort in 1968. Tom Terrific had 14 complete games, 5 shutouts and 205 strikeouts to go with his 2.20 ERA. Not too many hitters looked forward to facing either of the young Met pitchers.

The biggest problem was offense, power offense to be exact. Ed Charles, not a home run hitter, led the club with 15 round-trippers. Swoboda had the most RBIs with 59, while Jones was the leading hitter at .297. Agee was a disappointment his first year with the club and a couple of the other youngsters just didn't produce enough with the stick.

In late September, the team had an unexpected shock when manager Hodges suffered a mild heart attack. But he seemed to make a rapid recovery and doctors soon gave him full clearance to manage again in 1969. As that season approached, Mets fans thought about the manager's health and the health of their team. With luck, maybe the ball club would finally reach the .500 mark, or even beyond.

But even in the wildest dreams of the most enthused of Mets fans, no one was prepared for what was about to happen in the upcoming season.

team, looking to blend young players with some solid, role-playing veterans. In fact, there were probably more changes made between 1967 and 1968 than ever before in the team's brief history.

With Seaver as a cornerstone, they began to assemble a real pitching staff and it began with another major find. Jerry Koosman was a 24-year-old left-hander who had come up briefly at the tail end of 1967. He was 0-2 in 9 appearances with 3 starts. But when he returned in 1968, he looked just as good as Seaver. Suddenly the team had a potential righty-lefty, one-two punch to anchor their staff.

Another trio of youngsters – Dick Selma, Jim McAndrew, and Nolan Ryan – were also on the staff. Ryan was another poten-

Above: *Centerfielder Tommie Agee came to the Mets in a 1968 trade and was one of the heroes of the 1969 title team. Agee had speed and power at the plate and played a sometimes spectacular centerfield.*

Left: *Manager Hodges puts rookie pitcher Jerry Koosman through a workout at Shea in the spring of 1968. Koosman would win 19 games as a rookie and follow that with 17 more wins in the World Series season of 1969.*

3. The Miracle Mets

The 1969 season saw baseball expand once again. Two new teams joined both the National and American Leagues and led to a complete restructuring of the game. Each league was broken up into two divisions, the East and the West, with six teams in each. Divisional winners would now have to face each other in a best of five playoff series to determine the pennant winners.

Playing in the National League East, the Mets would be up against the Cubs, Pirates, Cards, Phils and the expansion Montreal Expos. They would, of course, also be playing the teams in the NL West.

Hodges and Murphy had essentially the same team as in 1968. But they did some fine tuning. Young right-hander Gary Gentry joined the team with the hope he could do what Seaver and Koosman had done in each of the previous two seasons. Lefty Tug McGraw was back as a relief specialist after a stint in the minors. Young third baseman Wayne Garrett joined the team, as did outfielder Rod Gaspar.

The team really wasn't complete until June 15. That's when the Mets acquired slugging first baseman Donn Clendenon from the Montreal Expos in exchange for four young players. Clendenon gave the club experience and a bona fide power hitter. Now Hodges could really plan his strategy. He decided to platoon at certain positions and stick to it throughout the rest of the season. Only outfielders Jones and Agee, catcher Grote and shortstop Harrelson could be considered every day players.

Before the season started, most so-called experts still picked the Mets to finish in the bottom half of their division. Only the eternal optimist Seaver saw it differently. Said Tom Terrific to anyone who would listen:

"You know, if we all play up to our potential we could win our division."

But during the early going not much seemed different. The ball club was below .500 and it was the Chicago Cubs that broke out of the gate quickly and had the early lead in the NL East race. On paper, the Mets didn't match up with the Cubs offensively. And if their pitching was better, it wasn't *that much* better. So with a slow start, there was little hope that the New Yorkers would recover enough to become a

Below left: *Tom Seaver is flanked by Ken Boswell (l) and Donn Clendenon after Tom Terrific beat the Cubs, 7-1, on September 9, 1969, bringing the Mets to within a half game of first place.*

Below right: *Aptly nicknamed "The Franchise," Tom Seaver was the Mets ace from his rookie year. Here, he delivers to Maury Wills of the expansionist Montreal Expos early in 1969.*

contender. Even when the team got its record up to .500 at 18-18 in May, there was little reason to get excited because they soon started to lose again.

On May 28, however, they broke a five-game losing streak with a victory. A day later Jerry Koosman, who had some arm trouble in the early going, fanned 15 Padres in ten innings and the Mets won it in the eleventh, 1-0, on a Bud Harrelson home run. Next the Giants and Dodgers were due to come into town. Up to that time, the return of the former New York franchises always spelled doom for the young Mets. But this time the Mets swept both former New York clubs, bringing their winning streak to seven straight. And it wasn't over yet.

The team flew to the West Coast where they whipped the Padres for three more, then beat the Giants for their eleventh straight victory, a new club record. Though the Giants stopped the streak the next day,

Above: *The Mets really put things together in 1969. Shortstop Bud Harrelson fires to first, completing a nifty double play in a game against the San Diego Padres.*

Above: *The scoreboard at Shea tells it all. On September 10, 1969, the Mets swept a pair from the Expos. Coupled with a Cubs loss, the Mets moved into first place for the first time in the team's history.*

shoulder stiffness. Tom Terrific wouldn't miss a turn, but would lose four of his next five decisions.

Mediocre baseball continued into August. By the 13th of the month, things looked bleak. Not only had the Mets just been swept 3 games by Houston, but they were suddenly in third place behind the Cardinals and 9½ games behind the front-running Cubs. It would have been easy at this point for the Mets to quit.

But prodded by manager Hodges and some of the veteran players, the team slowly came alive again. The stiffness had left Seaver's shoulder and the ace was back on a 20-victory pace again. The timely hitting had also returned. It wasn't just one or two players. Everyone seemed to take a turn. One day it was Jones, another Swoboda, then Kranepool, then Clendenon, then Agee.

In late August, the team went on another hot streak, winning 12 of 13 games. At the same time, the Cubs seemed to flounder. By September 1, the Mets were back in second place and had whittled the lead down to a scant 4 games. Pennant fever broke out all over again.

On September 4, Tom Seaver became the first Met pitcher ever to win 20 games. There had been many 20-game losers in the franchise's short history, so Tom Terrific was pleased to reverse that ignominious trend. What's more, the team continued to win. When the Cubs came into Shea for a crucial two-game series on September 8, they held just a 2½ game lead over the charging Mets.

In the opener, Koosman took the mound and came away with a 3-2 victory. Now the lead was 1½ games. And when Seaver pitched the team to a 7-1 win the next night, the Cubs' lead was scarcely visible at one-half game. The Cinderella Mets were on the threshhold of going into first place.

The very next night the Montreal Expos were at Shea for a twi-night doubleheader, while the Cubs were in Philadelphia for a single game. It was September 10, 1969, a date that will forever live in Mets' history. The Mets took the first game from Montreal, 3-2, and the minute it ended, at 8:43 P.M., they jumped into the lead by percentage points over the Cubs. It was the first time that this team, created to replace the Dodgers and Giants, had ever been in first place.

It all seemed even more real when the Mets won the second game, 7-1, and the Cubbies lost to the Phillies, 6-2. The Mets now had an 84-57 record to the Cubs' 84-59. They were in first by a full game.

Once the Mets took over the lead there was no stopping them. They won 13 of 14, 29

the Mets were nevertheless in second place, still far behind the Cubs, but six games ahead of the third-place Cardinals. Though it was hard for some to admit, the Mets were over .500 and suddenly contenders.

Several days after the winning streak ended, the Mets made the trade with Montreal for Donn Clendenon. The big slugger was sure to help in the power department, one area that still saw the Mets lacking. With the pitching looking even better than expected, the Mets began to believe they could make a real run at it. And pretty soon their fans were believing it as well.

When the Cubs came into Shea Stadium for a three-game set on July 8, they led the Mets by just five games. New York took two of three, rallying in the ninth to win the first game, then taking the second as Tom Seaver threw a one-hitter after coming within two outs of pitching a perfect game. Now the Amazing Mets were just four games from the top.

A week later, the Mets again won two of three from the Chicagoans and going into the All-Star break the New Yorkers were looking more and more like real contenders. It was obviously a different Mets team than their fans had ever seen before.

After the All-Star break, however, the ball club suddenly went into a slump. Seaver, their ace, who had been a brilliant 14-3 at one point, was complaining of of 36. With just 10 days remaining in the season they led the Cubs by 4½ games, so they still couldn't let down. But with the kind of magic they had been producing since mid-August, a letdown seemed rather unlikely.

It didn't happen. On September 24, the Mets shut out the Cards, 6-0, to clinch the National League Eastern Division title. They were champions, coming from ninth place all the way to first in a single year. It marked one of the great turnarounds in baseball history. When the season ended the Mets had a 100-62 record, finishing 8 games ahead of the Cubs, 12 ahead of the Pirates and 13 in front of the fourth-place Cardinals. They had blown away three of the best veteran teams in the division.

There were some great individual heroics as well. Seaver finished the year with a 25-7 record and a 2.21 earned run average. He would win the Cy Young Award as the best pitcher in the National League. Koosman wasn't very far behind. After shaking his early season arm trouble, the hard-throwing lefty wound up at 17-9 with a 2.28 ERA. Rookie Gentry was 13-12, while relievers McGraw and Taylor were 9-3 and 9-4 respectively, notching 25 saves between them. Cal Koonce and young Nolan Ryan were both 6-3, a far cry from when all the Mets' pitchers sported losing records.

The hitting wasn't great, but as a team the New Yorkers were more than adequate. Cleon Jones had some late-season injuries, but still finished at .340 to lead the team. He had 12 homers and 75 RBIs. Agee had 26 homers and 76 ribbies to go with a .271 average. Shamsky hit an even .300 with 14 homers, while Kranepool had 11 homers and 49 ribbies, and Swoboda belted 9 and added 52 RBIs. Newcomer Clendenon finished with 12 round-trippers and 37 RBIs platooning with Kranepool.

So it really was a team effort, led by outstanding pitching and timely hitting. Only the team wouldn't be going right to the World Series. Because it was the first year of divisional play, the Mets would have to meet the Western Division winner in a best of five series. That meant the Atlanta Braves, a team that had a 93-69 record for the regular season.

The Braves were a hard-hitting team led by the likes of the great Henry Aaron, Orlando Cepeda, Rico Carty, Filipe Alou, and Clete Boyer. They had a 23-game winner in Phil Niekro, but it was acknowledged that their pitching could not compare with that of the Mets. But were the Mets' hurlers good enough to silence the Atlanta bats? That question was answered quickly, as the Mets proved once and for all that in 1969 they were indeed for real.

It took the New Yorkers just three quick games to defeat the Braves and win the National League pennant. And they did it by outhitting the normally hard-hitting Braves. The scores were 9-5, 11-6, and 7-4, as the club won the first two at Atlanta and then came home to Shea for the clincher.

With the final out, the fans at Shea Stadium went wild. It was as if they were released from seven years of frustration, seven years of watching their team lose and become the laughingstock of all baseball. Now, the laughingstock was headed for the World Series and the fans responded by partying right out on the field, tearing up huge chunks of turf and leaving the field looking like a war zone.

The grounds crew had eight days to get the field in shape for the third game of the World Series. The first two would be played in ballpark of the American League champion, the Baltimore Orioles, considered by

Top: There's total joy in Metsville after Gary Gentry (hatless in center) shut out the Cardinals, 6-0, to clinch the Eastern Division title for the Mets on September 24, 1969.

Above: The Mets made another record the day after clinching the divisional title, this one in a recording studio. Taking part in the merriment are (l to r), Art Shamsky, Donn Clendenon, Rod Gaspar, Ken Boswell and Tug McGraw.

Above: *Mets owner Mrs. Joan Payson was a familiar figure around Shea Stadium until her death in 1975. She was one of baseball's most popular and beloved owners. Here, Mrs. Payson captures the flavor of her favorite team during the 1969 World Series.*

most as far and away the best team in all of baseball.

Baltimore had won 109 games during the regular season, finishing 19 games ahead of the Detroit Tigers in the AL East. Then they destroyed the Minnesota Twins in three straight playoff games. The Orioles came into the series with a balance of hitting and pitching that seemed tough to beat.

Lefties Mike Cuellar and Dave McNally were both 20-game winners, while righties Jim Palmer and Tom Phoebus won 16 and 14 respectively. Eddie Watt, Dick Hall, and Pete Richert combined for 34 bullpen saves and had a combined earned run average under 2.00.

Offensively, the team was also double trouble. First baseman John "Boog" Powell had his best year, hitting .304 with 37 homers and 121 RBIs. Veteran Frank Robinson was still a force with 32 homers and 100 ribbies to go with a .308 average. Centerfielder Paul Blair blasted 26 dingers and drove home 76 runs, while third sacker Brooks Robinson, the magician with the glove, found time to slam 23 homers and drive home 84 runs. Shortstop Mark Belanger, second baseman Davey Johnson, leftfielder Don Buford, and catcher Elrod Hendricks rounded out the starting lineup. The Orioles not only had thunder in their bats, but speed as well. And under fiery manager Earl Weaver they had put it together well.

Despite the feeling that the "Miracle" Mets were a "Team of Destiny," the Orioles were made heavy favorites to win the Series. The outstanding Mets pitching had faltered against the Braves. If it didn't rebound against the Orioles, the fall classic could be over quickly. Not surprisingly, Tom Seaver was named to start the opener. The 25-game winner would be opposed by the crafty Cuellar, who had won 23 in his own right.

After Cuellar retired the Mets in the first, Seaver took the mound to face Orioles leadoff hitter Don Buford. On Tom Terrific's second pitch, Buford swung and hit a high drive over the rightfield wall for a home run. The Baltimore fans went crazy as Buford circled the bases. Seaver just kicked at the rubber. He couldn't believe the lead-off hitter had smacked one out. But he also knew there was plenty of time for the Mets to get back into the game.

Only the New Yorkers weren't doing anything with the southpaw offerings of Mike Cuellar. The crafty veteran kept them off balance through the first four innings. Then in the bottom of the fourth, the Orioles went to work on Seaver again, scoring 3 more runs to make it a 4-0 game. Cuellar made the 4-0 score stand up, weakening

only briefly in the seventh when Al Weis's sacrifice fly gave the Mets their only run.

Could the Mets rebound? They would have to do it quickly. To be down two games to a team like the Orioles would give them a mighty high mountain to climb. Jerry Koosman would be on the mound for the New Yorkers in game two, and he would be opposed by 20-game winner Dave McNally.

For three innings, the two southpaws were in command, neither team doing any

damage. But in the fourth, Donn Clendenon took McNally downtown, slamming a home run over the left centerfield fence. The Mets had a 1-0 lead, the first time they were on top in the Series.

It was still a 1-0 game after six and almost as significant as the score was the fact that the Orioles had yet to get a base hit. The chance of a no-hitter ended in the seventh when Paul Blair singled up the middle. Then, after the Mets lefty retired

Frank Robinson and Powell, Blair stole second and scampered home on a single by Brooks Robinson. The game was now tied at 1-1.

By the ninth inning it was still knotted at 1-1. McNally retired the first two Mets, but then singles by Charles and Grote put runners on first and second. Al Weis then poked a McNally offering for a single that scored Charles. So the Mets had a 2-1 lead as the Birds came up for the final time.

Above: *Baltimore lefty Mike Cuellar fires the first pitch of the 1969 World Series. The game was played at Baltimore's Memorial Stadium and the leadoff hitter is Tommie Agee.*

Above right:
*Southpaw Jerry
Koosman was the
Mets' best pitcher in
the 1969 Series. He
defeated the Orioles
twice, including the
fifth and final game
that made the New
Yorkers world
champs.*

Far right: *Tommie
Agee makes the first
of two sensational
catches in the third
game of the Series,
won by the Mets, 5-0.
Agee's pair of gems
saved at least 5 runs
and maybe the game.*

But there was more to it than that. During game three the Mets were beginning to show that perhaps they were a team of destiny after all. Two brilliant catches by Tommie Agee saved at least five Oriole runs. Agee made a last-second backhanded catch at the left centerfield fence in the fourth, then made a diving grab in right center in the sixth.

Now it was Seaver and Cuellar matching up again in the fourth game and this one was a dandy. The Mets got a run in the second when Clendenon slammed one into the leftfield bullpen for his second homer of the Series. The 1-0 score stood up all the way into the ninth inning. Tom Seaver was just three outs away from a complete game shutout.

He got Blair to open the inning, but then Frank Robinson and Powell both singled, putting runners on first and third and bringing up the always-dangerous Brooks Robinson. A tiring Seaver knew the Met bullpen was working behind him, but he wanted to try to nail it down. He threw Robinson a low fastball and the Orioles great third sacker drilled it. It was a sink-

Koosman quickly retired the first two hitters, but then he wavered and walked both Frank Robinson and Powell. Manager Hodges then brought in righty reliever Ron Taylor to face the dangerous Brooks Robinson. Taylor got Robby to bounce to third for the final out. The Mets had won it, 2-1, evened the Series, and would now be returning to Shea.

Rookie Gary Gentry faced the Orioles' Jim Palmer in game three. This one was all Mets. Agee belted a homer leading off the first. In the second, pitcher Gentry whacked a two-out double to drive in a pair and give the Mets a 3-0 lead. Single runs in the sixth and eighth made it 5-0 and that's the way it ended. Gentry had pitched into the seventh and was relieved by Nolan Ryan with two outs. Ryan then completed the shutout and the Mets had a 2-1 Series lead.

Left: *Jerry Koosman is flanked by Cleon Jones (l) and Donn Clendenon following the lefty's 2-hit, 2-1 victory in game two of the Series. Clendenon contributed a big home run.*

ing line drive into right center. If it fell, the Orioles would have the lead.

A diving, sprawling catch by rightfielder Swoboda saved the day. Though Frank Robinson tagged up and trotted home with the tying run, Swoboda had saved at least one more from scoring. Seaver then bore down and retired Ellie Hendricks, but when the Mets couldn't score in their half of the ninth, the game went to extra innings tied at 1-1.

Seaver hoped he had one more inning in him. He did, retiring the Orioles in the tenth. Jerry Grote led off the last of the tenth against reliever Dick Hall and lifted a lazy fly to left. Buford lost the ball in the late-afternoon sun and it fell for a double. Rod Gaspar pinch ran for Grote and then Al Weis walked. Reserve catcher J.C. Martin came up to bat for Seaver as lefty Pete Richert took over on the mound. It was a bunt situation and Martin laid one down the first-base line.

Richert pounced off the mound to get the ball and throw to first. But his throw never made it. It hit the runner Martin on the arm and bounced into the outfield. The speedy Gaspar took advantage of the situation and sped home with the winning run! Now the Mets were just one game away from being World Series champions.

The baseball world was stunned by what was happening. In the eyes of most, the Orioles were the best. Yet the Mets, a team many thought didn't really belong there despite their heroics, had won three straight games and were on the brink of making diamond history. Game five would see Koosman taking the mound for the Mets against Dave McNally of the Birds.

Orioles fans were still waiting for the big bats to erupt. But in the first two innings of game five, nothing happened. Then, in the top of the third, Baltimore broke through against Koosman, scoring three times and jumping in front, 3-0. Maybe the hard-hitting Birds were finally going to snap out of it?

But the Orioles weren't about to drive Koosman to the showers. The young left-hander quickly settled down and retired the next eight Orioles in order before giving up a harmless single in the sixth. The Mets, in the meantime, had done little with Dave McNally. And as they came to bat in the

Below: *The Mets scored the winning run in the tenth inning of game four. J.C. Martin (9) bunted to Oriole pitcher Pete Richert with runners on first and second. Richert's throw to first hit Martin and bounced away from the O's Davey Johnson, allowing Rod Gaspar to score.*

Right: *Manager Gil Hodges shows umpire Lou DiMuro a smudge of shoe polish on the ball that proved Cleon Jones had been hit by a pitched ball in the sixth inning of game five. Jones went to first and the next hitter, Donn Clendenon, promptly whacked a homer.*

Below: *Donn Clendenon's big swing produced the home run that propelled the Mets to a world's championship in game five.*

bottom of the sixth they knew it was time to get something started.

Leadoff hitter Cleon Jones tried to get away from a low inside pitch, which he claimed hit him on the foot. When plate umpire Lou DiMuro said no, manager Hodges came out, retrieved the ball and showed the ump a smudge of shoe polish that he felt proved the ball had hit Jones's foot. DiMuro agreed and Cleon took first.

Donn Clendenon was next and he promptly sent a McNally pitch over the centerfield wall for his third homer of the Series. That made the score 3-2. The Mets were coming back. An inning later, the Mets pulled even when the usually weak-hitting Al Weis sent a McNally curveball over the leftfield wall. Weis's surprise homer renewed thoughts of destiny. To many fans at Shea Stadium, the Mets simply couldn't lose.

Koosman continued his mastery by shutting down the Orioles in the top of the eighth. Now the Mets came up with visions of champagne dancing in their eyes. A pair of runs gave the Mets a 5-3 lead and the Orioles had just three outs left.

The young left-hander took a deep breath and went to work. He tried to be too fine with Frank Robinson and walked him. But then he got Powell to hit into a fielder's choice and Brooks Robinson to fly to right for the second out. With the capacity crowd screaming and on its feet, second baseman Davey Johnson was up. Koosman dealt and Johnson lofted a lazy fly toward left. Cleon Jones tapped his glove and made the catch, dropping to one knee as he did. Jones held that pose for a second, as if in prayer, and as he rose the whole place erupted.

The Mets had done it. They were World Series champions!

Below: *The Miracle Mets win the Series and it's pandemonium for players and fans alike after the final out of game five. After losing the first game, the Mets took four straight to beat the powerful Orioles and the fans celebrated by tearing the Shea Stadium turf apart.*

4. On Top of the World

Below: *Baseball's best in 1969, the New York Mets, World Champs.*

Opposite: *New York City opened its hearts to the champion Mets, the perennial underdogs who made good. Jerry Koosman (l) and Tom Seaver enjoy part of a great tickertape parade for the team in lower Manhattan.*

The celebration was nothing less than titanic. New York City treated its champions as old-fashioned heroes. The Mets were, not surprisingly, the absolute toast of the town. There were all kinds of ceremonies including a huge tickertape parade. The miracle of a team that had never finished higher than ninth in its history suddenly winning it all escaped no one. It was the sports story of the year.

Almost every sportswriter, broadcaster, media buff, and man on the street tried to analyze the Mets' meteoric rise. It wasn't an easy thing to do. After all, how do you explain perennial doormats suddenly becoming world beaters? There didn't seem to be one set answer. However, the only way the Mets could prove they were truly a great team was to repeat, or at least come close to repeating. Could they stay at or near the top for a number of years? This was the question being asked of the Mets shortly after the Series ended.

That's why 1970 was looked upon as a key year for the entire team. There were a few minor changes in personnel, but the one thing that bothered some people was the quick release of veteran third sacker Ed Charles after the Series ended. Charles was a fine fielder and while he didn't do much with the stick, was one of the "up" guys in the clubhouse and was really loved by the other players.

Joe Foy, a young third baseman of sup-

Above: *Jack Lang (l) and Mets general manager Bob Scheffing (r) present Tom Seaver with the Cy Young Award for 1969. There was little doubt that the 25-7 Seaver was the National League's best hurler that season.*

posedly unlimited potential, was acquired from Kansas City to take Charles's place. One of the players sent to K.C. was minor league outfielder Amos Otis, who would become a longtime American League star. It was the first of several disastrous deals that would mark the Mets of the 1970s.

Then in January of 1970, the team suffered a tragic loss with the sudden death of general manager Johnny Murphy from a heart attack. It may have been a sign of things to come because the Mets of 1970 failed to recapture the magic of the year before. The team hung in the race, but only because no one else was strong enough to break away from the pack. But for much of the year the battle was simply to get above the .500 mark.

On April 22, Tom Seaver again showed why he was one of the great young pitchers in baseball. Facing the San Diego Padres, Tom Terrific tied a major league record by striking out 19 hitters. And by fanning the final 10 Padres in succession, he set a brand new mark of his own. It was an overpowering performance and at the time fans hoped it would light a fire under the team.

But the first half of the season was one of streaks, wins and losses often coming in bunches. Koosman was having some arm problems again, Gentry was no more than a .500 pitcher and Ryan was still inconsistent. Only Seaver was doing the job with 14 wins by the All-Star break. And the club was still hanging tough in second place, a

game and a half behind the Pirates. Maybe the Mets could recapture the magic and produce another second-half surge as they had done the year before.

But there was no surge. By mid-August, the club still trailed the Pirates by two and a half. Seaver was 17-6 then and a decision was made to pitch the ace with only three days rest. That's when Tom Terrific lost three straight. It was the start of a streak that would see him win only one more time while losing six and finish with an 18-12 record. A tired arm? Maybe. But without Tom Seaver winning down the stretch, the Mets just didn't have enough.

Koosman again came on late and kept the Mets in the race. But the Pirates beat the Mets three of four in mid-September, then swept them three straight with just a week left in the season and that about did it. The New Yorkers wound up with an 83-79 record, just four games over .500, and finished third, six games behind Pittsburgh and one in back of the Cubs. There would be no miracles in 1970.

Despite his slump Seaver finished 18-12 with a 2.81 earned run average and led the National League with 283 strikeouts. Koosman's strong finish left him at 12-7, but he had now experienced arm trouble two years in a row. Gentry was just 9-9 and Ryan 7-11. Another young starter, Jim McAndrew, was 10-14. Where had all the pitching gone?

Some of the hitters did well. Clendenon

smacked 22 homers and drove home 97 runs, while Agee hit 24 and drove in 75. Jones average, however, fell from .340 to .277, though Cleon helped with 63 ribbies. But Joe Foy was a big disappointment at third and players like Boswell, Swoboda, and Kranepool didn't seem to be getting much better. They would not be major stars.

Maybe that's why 1971 was almost a carbon copy of 1970. The club again finished at 83-79, tied with the Cubs for third in the division, but this time 14 games behind the winning Pirates. The offense was just mediocre and the pitching also left questions. Seaver was brilliant again, finishing at 20-10 with a microscopic 1.76 earned run average, best in the league. His 289 strikeouts were also tops in the circuit. McGraw was also outstanding in the pen, with an 11-4 record and 1.70 ERA. But Koosman was just 6-11 (arm trouble again), Gentry 12-11, Ryan 10-14. Suddenly, there weren't enough reliable arms. It was beginning to look as if a major overhaul might be needed.

There was one major change prior to the 1972 season, however, that nobody anticipated or wanted to see. On April 2, at the tail end of spring training and with the players gone because of a brief strike, manager Hodges suddenly collapsed and died of a massive heart attack. Though he had had a mild heart attack several years earlier, the Met manager seemed in good health and his death came as a shock to the team, to baseball, and to the city of New York, where he had played with the Dodgers for so long.

With the season ready to begin, the team had to regroup and quickly named coach Yogi Berra the new manager. Like Hodges, Yogi was extremely popular with New York sports fans. He was a Hall of Fame catcher with the Yankees and had managed the Bombers briefly, winning the pennant with them in 1964. So he did bring some experience to the job.

The team also made some major deals. Rusty Staub, a good hitting outfielder and leader came over from Montreal in return for three young prospects – Tim Foli, Ken Singleton, and Mike Jorgensen. And in another trade, the erratic Nolan Ryan was sent to the California Angels in return for veteran shortstop Jim Fregosi, who would play third for the Mets. That one could qualify as one of the five worst trades in the history of the game. Fregosi fizzled while Ryan became the game's greatest strikeout pitcher and a star performer who would throw effectively into his forties.

And in May, the team really brought a star home. Willie Mays, the great New York and San Francisco Giant, joined the Mets. Though in the twilight of his Hall of Fame career, Mays was a fan attraction and a ballplayer who could still on occasion turn back the clock. He would only be a part-timer, but everyone felt it was fitting for the

Above: *Jerry Koosman showing his form. Before arm problems slowed him down, many felt that Koosman was the equal of Seaver and that the two young pitchers were the best righty-lefty combo in baseball.*

Right: *Willie Mays returns to New York sporting a Mets uniform.*

Below: *The Mets made a major trade with the Expos early in 1972, acquiring top hitter Rusty Staub (l) for three young prospects: (t to b) Ken Singleton, Tim Foli and Mike Jorgensen.*

"Say Hey Kid" to end his career back in New York. When Willie got on base 14 times in his first 27 at bats as a Met, all looked right with the world.

With all these changes, the ball club got off fast. An 11-game winning streak helped the team to a 30-11 start that saw them take a 5-game lead by June 1. Seaver was pitching well and getting unexpected support from a rookie left-hander, Jon Matlack. He had taken up some of the slack left by Koosman's arm troubles. Jerry did not have the old power and was trying to readjust as a pitcher.

As June passed, the Mets found themselves coming back to the pack. There were some injuries and some inconsistencies. Staub was hitting well, Fregosi wasn't. Both Agee and Jones, still young players, seemed to have lost something and were not having good years. Rookie first baseman John Milner was supplying some unexpected power, but it just wasn't a complete and solid team.

By the end of June, the Mets found themselves trailing the Pirates, and by late July they were 5½ games behind. When it ended, the club was in third place, finishing at 83-73, 13½ games behind the division-winning Pirates. The Cubs were second, 2½ in front of the Mets. Though the team again finished above .500, it was a disappointing year in many ways.

Seaver won 21 games, Matlack 15, but Gentry at 7-10 and Koosman at 11-12 were disappointments. Milner led the club in homers with 17, Staub led in hitting at .293 despite missing a good part of the year with an injury, and Jones led in RBIs with only 52. With the pitching a bit thin and the offense anemic, the Mets did well to finish as high as they did.

Then came 1973, one of the strangest years in Mets history. The club added a solid second baseman in veteran Felix Millan. Tommie Agee was traded for not much in return and pitcher George Stone came over from the Braves. So it was essentially the same team with the same problems. Fortunately, for the Mets, it was a year in which all the teams in the National League East had one problem or another. In a nutshell, no one seemed to want to win the thing. Even manager Berra must have sensed it when he said: "It won't take more than 90 victories to win in this division. So if we can win 90 and don't have a lot of bad injuries . . ."

Early on, it didn't look real good. The team was inconsistent and the injuries were starting all over again. During the first half of the year Milner, Harrelson, Jones, Mays, and Grote all spent time on the disabled list. Rusty Staub's wrist still

Above: *Rusty Staub falls down but still holds onto the ball after slamming into the wall following a spectacular catch.*

Far left: *Lefthander Jon Matlack was Rookie of the Year in 1972 when he was 15-10 for the Mets.*

Left: *Veteran southpaw George Stone came to the Mets in 1973 and went 12-3.*

Above: *Relief ace Tug McGraw keyed the drive to the pennant in 1973 when he coined the phrase, "You gotta believe!" The emotional lefthander also pitched extremely well during the stretch drive.*

ached after a fracture the year before. And while the starting pitching was solid, reliever Tug McGraw was struggling.

By mid-June, the team was battling to stay at .500 as they sat in third place, 6½ games behind the Cubs. But even as the injured players began to return after the All-Star break, the Mets couldn't really pick up the pace. In August, they were below .500 and things looked very bleak. In fact, on August 5, they fell all the way to last place, 11½ games out of first.

Then, they slowly began showing signs of life. Reliever Tug McGraw finally found the groove and also coined the rallying cry for the entire team when he proclaimed:

"You gotta believe!"

On August 20 the club was still last, though the entire National League East pack had tightened up. That led the ever

optimistic McGraw to say, "We might be the first club in last place on August 20th to win a pennant. Last place to first place in six weeks! Wouldn't that be something?"

It wasn't just an impossible dream. None of the other teams seemed to have the talent to blow the race open. By September 1, the New Yorkers were still 10 games below .500 at 61-71. Then with McGraw again becoming the stopper out of the pen, the walking wounded back in action, and Seaver, Koosman, Matlack, and Stone all pitching well, the Mets suddenly began to play like it was 1969 all over again. On September 21, Seaver pitched the team to a 10-2 victory over the Pirates, putting the Amazins into first place. But with the final week of the season approaching, five of the six teams were still within 3½ games of each other.

Finally, the Mets went into Chicago for the last four games of the year. They had just a half game lead on the Pirates, so the pressure was on. This one would definitely go down to the wire. And oddly enough, the four games were scheduled as two double-headers on Sunday and Monday.

The Mets lost the first Sunday game, 1-0, as Rick Reuschel bested Matlack. More pressure. But in the second game the offense came alive and Koosman coasted, 9-2. Now there were two games left. If the Mets won just one of them, they would take the division title.

Seaver started the first game, and thanks to Cleon Jones's homer and a bases loaded single by Jerry Grote, the Mets had a 3-0 lead in the fourth. They made it 5-0 in the fifth, but the Cubs closed to 5-2 and then 5-4. Then McGraw came on and pitched as he had all during September. He was superb, getting the save as the Mets won 6-4, to clinch the National League East title. Four years after the miracle of 1969, the New York Mets had done it again!

The 1973 Mets were not a great baseball team. They won the division with an 82-79 mark, just three games over .500 and topping the 81-81 Cards by just 1½ games. But they had enough talent and drive to win 29 of their final 43 contests and 20 of their last 28. And in a division where no team seemed to get hot, that was just enough.

Seaver was perhaps the only individual player to have an outstanding year. Tom Terrific was 19-10 with a league-leading 2.08 earned run average and a National League best 251 strikeouts. He would later win his second Cy Young Award for his efforts. Koosman finished at 14-15, but with a fine, 2.84 ERA, while Matlack was 14-16. Both would have done better with more support. Stone was the real surprise, compiling a 12-3 mark, while McGraw was just 5-6, but had 25 big saves, many of them coming in the stretch drive.

Felix Millan was the leading hitter at .290, while Milner topped the club with 23 homers and Staub led in RBIs with 76. Mays was at the end of his career and the rest of the offense was still weak. But the team would need all the firepower they could muster. For in the playoffs they would be meeting the powerful Cincinnati Reds, winners of 99 games during the regular season. The Reds were installed as overwhelming favorites for the best of five playoff series.

It wasn't hard to see why. Cincy had the likes of Pete Rose, Tony Perez, Joe Morgan, and Johnny Bench just for starters. The team could score runs in bunches. They also had a 19-game winner in Jack Billingham and an 18-game winner in Don Gullett.

Three other pitchers won more than 10 and Clay Carroll and Pedro Borbon had 14 saves apiece out of the bullpen. The Reds had also been to the World Series in 1970 and 1972, losing both times. So the team was hungry for a world title. On paper, the championship series looked like no contest.

The playoff series went the full five games, with both teams battling to the hilt. But in the end it was the superior Mets pitching that shut down the big bats of the Reds. The Mets hoped to wrap it up in four, but the great Pete Rose belted a twelfth-inning homer to win that game and add to

Top: *Following the 1973 season Tom Seaver won his second Cy Young Award as the best pitcher in the National League.*

Above: *Tug McGraw is congratulated by John Milner as the Mets beat the Cubs, 6-4, to clinch another divisional title.*

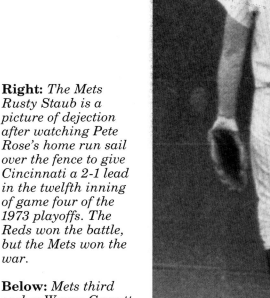

Right: *The Mets Rusty Staub is a picture of dejection after watching Pete Rose's home run sail over the fence to give Cincinnati a 2-1 lead in the twelfth inning of game four of the 1973 playoffs. The Reds won the battle, but the Mets won the war.*

Below: *Mets third sacker Wayne Garrett shows his batting form during the playoff series against the Reds.*

drama. Fittingly, it was Tom Seaver who finally nailed it down. With ninth-inning help from Tug McGraw, The Franchise topped the Reds, 7-2, to give the Mets their second National League pennant.

Once again they had done it in miraculous fashion, nearly as miraculous as in 1969. Only this time they entered the Series with a .509 winning percentage in the regular season, the lowest of any team ever going to the fall classic.

That would make it tough. After all, now the Mets would have to face the defending world champion Oakland A's. The A's had disposed of the Baltimore Orioles in the playoffs and were a very strong team. They had a trio of 20-game winners in Catfish Hunter, Vida Blue, and Ken Holtzman as well as a pair of ace relievers in Rollie Fingers and Darold Knowles.

The offense was led by league homer and RBI king Reggie Jackson, Sal Bando, Gene Tenace, Joe Rudi, and Deron Johnson. Like the Reds, Oakland was capable of heavy-duty offense at any time. Once again the Mets were the underdogs, but they were getting used to playing that role and seemed to relish in it.

Game one saw Matlack facing Holtzman. This one was a pitcher's battle and was won by the A's, 2-1, when the normally sure-handed Felix Millan made an error that

Left: *An unhappy Tom Seaver turns his back as Oakland's Bert Campaneris crosses home plate with the tying run in game three of the 1973 World Series. The A's won it in the eleventh.*

allowed the winning run to score. The Mets tried to get even by throwing Jerry Koosman against the A's in the second game. He was opposed by Vida Blue in a battle of southpaws. This one wasn't a pitcher's battle. On the contrary, it was a four-hour donnybrook that went twelve innings, with the Mets winning it 10-7 with 4 runs in the twelfth.

Now as the two teams flew cross-country to New York, it was all even at a game apiece. And in the third game Seaver took to the hill against the always tough Jim "Catfish" Hunter. The Mets got a pair of runs in the first, but the A's chipped away with a run in the sixth and another in the eighth. For the second day in a row the game went into extra innings and this time the A's won it in the eleventh inning as shortstop Bert Campaneris got the big hit off Harry Parker.

But with the Mets' strong pitching they could never be counted out. Matlack took over the next day and got major support from Rusty Staub, who slammed a 3-run homer in the first and later added 3 singles and another pair of RBIs in a 6-1 victory. So once again the two teams were tied and now the fifth game became the pivotal one. It would be Jerry Koosman and Vida Blue opposing each other for the second time.

As had been the case so often since 1969, it was Mets pitching that dominated a big game. Blue did a good job, but the New Yorkers touched him for a run in the second on a Cleon Jones double and for one more in the sixth on a triple by the normally weak-hitting Don Hahn. Meanwhile Koosman was shutting down the A's and when the veteran lefty faltered in the seventh, McGraw came in to finish the job. Oakland managed just three hits and the Mets won,

Above: *Pitcher George Stone doffs his cap to the crowd after saving the second game of the 1973 Series for the Mets. The New Yorkers won in twelve innings, 10-7.*

2-0. As the teams returned to Oakland for game six, the Mets were on the verge of another world championship.

Only these Oakland A's didn't quit, either. The Mets sent Tom Seaver to the mound hoping that their ace could close it out. But Catfish Hunter and the A's had a different idea, and with support from "Mr. October," Reggie Jackson, Oakland evened the Series.

Jackson doubled in Joe Rudi in the first, then slammed another double in the third to drive home Sal Bando. Hunter made the 2-0 lead stand up through the seventh. In the top of the eighth the Mets got one back on three singles, but Oakland got an insurance run in the bottom of the inning when Jackson singled and eventually scored on a sacrifice fly by Jesus Alou. The 3-1 victory made it a one-game series, with Jon Matlack and Ken Holtzman taking the mound to decide it.

Neither team scored for two and a half innings. But in the bottom of the third, the Mets finally began running out of miracles. Pitcher Holtzman started things with a double down the leftfield line. Then Campaneris, not a big power hitter, slammed a Matlack offering over the rightfield fence for a 2-run homer. Still, the A's weren't finished. Rudi singled and after Bando popped out, Reggie Jackson connected for a long 2-run shot of his own. The A's jumped out in front, 4-0, and that would prove all they needed.

The A's had won their second of three successive championships, 5-2, as the Mets finally tasted defeat. There would be no tickertape parade this time for the team that had shocked the baseball world in 1969 and almost did it again four years later.

Little did anyone know then as the New Yorkers sadly left the Oakland Coliseum, but the Mets' first real era of success was about to end. In fact, the bubble was ready to burst and Mets fans would find themselves with little to cheer about for the better part of a decade.

Left: *Tug McGraw was the winning pitcher in game two of the 1973 Series. Tug is joined in the locker room by manager Yogi Berra and Willie Mays.*

Below: *The great Willie Mays's last major league at bat came when he pinch hit for Tug McGraw in the third game of the 1973 World Series.*

5. A Decade of Change and Frustration

Below: *Veteran hitting star Joe Torre dons a Mets jersey prior to the 1975 season. A former NL batting champ, Torre came over from the Cardinals and is joined by Mets manager Yogi Berra (l) and general manager Joe McDonald.*

The World Series loss of 1973 was naturally a big disappointment to the Mets' players and fans. But, in retrospect, the team had come a lot further than anyone could have predicted and in some ways it helped justify 1969. It took four years, but the Mets had shown they could win again with basically the same team.

Of course, whenever a team gets into the World Series, people expect them to do well again the next year. But the 1974 season didn't bode well from the beginning. Willie Mays had retired, the Say Hey Kid finally coming to the end of a long, Hall of Fame career.

What didn't change in 1974 was the basic ball club. There were no new faces, at least none that made significant contributions. And some of the young players like Boswell, Garrett, and Milner hadn't developed as had been hoped. Cleon Jones had problems staying healthy and hadn't become the kind of hitter he appeared to be in 1969. The New Yorkers also lacked a big power guy and when Tom Seaver had the first off-season of his career, the team nosedived.

Tom Terrific had an 11-11 record in 1974 and a 3.20 earned run average. Koosman rebounded to win 15, while Jon Matlack took 13 with 7 shutouts and a 2.41 ERA. But

there wasn't much hitting. Rusty Staub was the top power man with 19 homers and 78 RBIs. The result was a 71-91 record and fifth-place finish in the NL East, not a good situation for defending league champions. It was also a year in which the club played another of its marathon games, losing a 4-3, 25-inning decision to the Cardinals at Shea on September 11. The game was symbolic of the season – long and frustrating.

It was obvious the team could no longer stand pat. Centerfielder Del Unser and catcher John Stearns came over from the Phillies in a major deal that saw popular reliever Tug McGraw depart. The team also purchased the contract of moody and inconsistent slugger Dave Kingman from the Giants. Injuries would relegate Cleon Jones to only 21 games and it was beginning to look as if his Met days were numbered. Former batting champion Joe Torre also joined the team. But at age 35, Torre was probably no longer an everyday player.

The transformation of the team resulted in an 82-80 season, disappointing by most standards. Manager Berra was fired on August 6, with coach Roy McMillan handling the club for the balance of the year. Although there was a bit more offense in 1975, the real difference between the 71-91 of 1974 and the 82-80 of 1975 was in the performance of Tom Seaver.

Tom Terrific was once again the best pitcher in the National League, winning his third Cy Young Award on the basis of a 22-9 record, 243 strikeouts and a 2.38 earned run average. Seaver set a major league record by becoming the first pitcher ever to strike out 200 or more batters for 8 straight seasons. He was backed by Matlack at 16-12

Below left: *In 1975, the Mets family lost two beloved members. Team owner Mrs. Joan Payson (c) and former manager Casey Stengel both died during the offseason. The two are shown here in 1963, along with Casey's wife, Edna.*

Left: *Slugger Dave Kingman joined the Mets in 1975 and promptly set a team record for homers with 36.*

and Koosman at 14-13, but there wasn't much else. The second line pitching had slipped.

In the offensive department, Staub became the first Met to go over 100 RBIs with 105, while Kingman broke Frank Thomas's long-standing club record by belting 36 home runs. Ed Kranepool hit .323 in a part-time role, Unser batted .294, Millan .283 and Staub .282. Rookie outfielder Mike Vail came up late in the year and tied a club record with a 23-game hitting streak. So there was some offense, and maybe a glimmer of hope for 1976.

During the off-season, the club mourned the passing of two beloved figures, former manager Casey Stengel and popular team owner Joan Payson. So the next season

Above: *It's spring training, 1977, and Mets pitchers Jerry Koosman (r) and Skip Lockwood take a break to pose for a photo. The veteran Koosman had a 21-10 record in 1976.*

began with something of a pall hanging over the ball club. The new manager was longtime minor league skipper Joe Frazier, and one major change on the field saw the trading of Rusty Staub to the Detroit Tigers in return for former 20-game winner, southpaw Mickey Lolich. But like Joe Torre before him, Lolich was 35 and on the downside of his career when he joined the Mets.

On paper, the 1976 season wasn't a bad one. Seaver, Koosman, and Matlack still presented an imposing Big Three, and the club squeezed enough hitting out of the

offense to have a winning season. They were 86-76, good for third but a distant 15 games behind the Phillies, who won the division with 101 victories. And despite finishing 10 games over .500, their best record since 1969 and second best ever, the Mets were still seen by many as a team that could nosedive at any time. In other words, it wasn't a very stable 86-76.

Koosman led the pitching parade with his first 20-win season, finishing at 21-10 with a 2.70 ERA. Matlack was 17-10 with a 2.95 earned run average and a league leading 6 shutouts. Seaver tailed off to 14-11, but had the best ERA among the starters at 2.59 and extended his record by striking out more than 200 hitters for a 9th straight year. Lolich pitched well in spots, had some hard luck, and finished at 8-13.

Kingman set another team homer mark with 37 and drove home 86 runs. But Staub's production wasn't replaced, though Milner had 15 dingers and 78 ribbies. Veteran Ed Kranepool hit 10 homers and drove home 49, but no other player had more than 35 runs batted in. The team just didn't hit enough. Plus Koosman would be 34 and Seaver 33 before the 1977 season began. How much longer could they be expected to excel? And without that superb front-line pitching, the whole team could come crashing down. And that's just what happened in 1977, one of the strangest and most pivotal years in the history of the franchise.

The club had some new faces right off the bat. Rookie switch hitter Lee Mazzilli took over in centerfield and right-handers Craig Swan and Nino Espinosa joined the rotation as Lolich moved on. Yet the changes did nothing to alter the fortune of the club. It was downhill from the beginning, as team was flirting with the basement, a low-rent location they hadn't been in since 1967.

It didn't take long for move number one. Joe Frazier was dismissed as manager on May 31, replaced by Joe Torre, who became the first player-manager since Solly Hemus with the Cardinals back in 1959. Torre would keep both roles until June 18, when he would become strictly a manager. And by that time the greatest purge in the team's history had been completed.

Tom Seaver had been having some problems coming to terms on a new contract with the ball club with words between the two parties becoming harsh, and the three-time Cy Young Award winner often talking about going someplace else. Yet most fans felt the man they now called The Franchise would be a Met forever. But on June 15, there was a startling announcement that stood the baseball world on its ear.

Seaver had been traded to the Cincinnati Reds for four players – young right-hander

Left: *Joe Torre hits the phone after taking over at Mets manager in June of 1977.*

Below: *Manager Torre (c) greets four new Mets acquired in two dramatic June 1977 trades that sent Tom Seaver to Cincinnati and Dave Kingman to San Diego. They are: (l to r) Doug Flynn, Pat Zachry, Torre, Steve Henderson, and Bobby Valentine.*

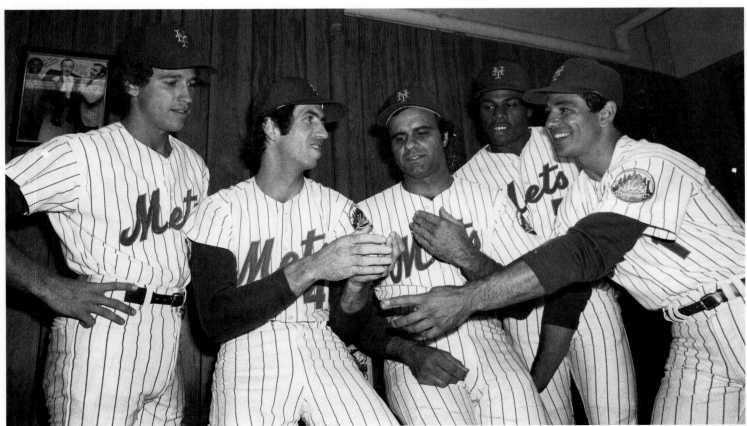

Pat Zachry, outfielders Steve Henderson and Dan Norman, and slick fielding infielder Doug Flynn. And that wasn't all. The same day the club announced that slugger Dave Kingman had been sent to San Diego in return for utility players Paul Siebert and Bobby Valentine. And to complete the day, the Mets acquired infielder-outfielder Joel Youngblood from the Cardinals.

Rarely has a team ever made such major roster changes in a single day. At a hastily convened news conference, a tearful Tom Seaver said goodbye to the fans of New York, adding that he hadn't wanted it to end this way. It was an emotional moment for one of the most popular and talented players in New York baseball history.

But how did the two major moves leave the Mets? After all, the team had dispensed with its best pitcher and top slugger in one move. It was hoped that Zachry, who was just 25 and 14-7 as a rookie a year earlier, would blossom into a star. And youngsters Espinosa and Swan would now get a chance to develop as well. While Norman went to the minors, Henderson played in left and the club hoped that in Henderson, Mazzilli, and Vail, they had a young outfield that could stay together for years.

Flynn and Youngblood contributed immediately as utility players, enabling manager Torre to take himself off the active roster. As it turned out, the young players did well, but the team never pulled itself out of the tailspin, finishing last with a 64-98 record.

Henderson hit 12 homers, drove in 65 runs and batted a solid .297 while finishing

Above: *Frank Cashen was named the Mets general manager in February 1980. Under Cashen, the Mets would become one of baseball's best teams in the middle and late 1980s.*

Right: *The day before the 1980 season opened, Shea Stadium was like a lake, prompting second baseman Doug Flynn to get out his fishing pole.*

Opposite: *Mookie Wilson was one of the Mets' new faces in the 1980s. Here, the fleet outfielder crosses the plate after belting a homer in a 1982 game against the Phils and is greeted by Ron Gardenhire.*

second to Montreal's Andre Dawson in the Rookie of the Year voting. Youngblood hit .253 and Flynn only .191 in limited appearances, while Zachry compiled just a 7-6 record after coming over to the Mets. Koosman went from 21-10 the year before to 8-20 in 1977, while Matlack fell to 7-15. Nino Espinosa was the top winner with 10 victories. Meanwhile Seaver, who was 7-3 at the time of the trade, pitched brilliantly for the Reds, winning 14 and losing just 3 with Cincy for a 21-6 overall mark. Tom was still pretty terrific and the Mets missed him.

It was a shaky rebuilding process and it was being reflected at the gate. The club drew 1,468,754 fans in 1976, lowest mark ever at Shea. Then in 1977, the crowds dwindled to 1,066,825. The 1978 season produced another last-place finish (66-96) and attendance of just 1,007,328 fans.

The year was disastrous in many ways. The numbers for both the pitchers and hitters seemed more like the mid-1960s, when the original Mets made a permanent home at basement level. When a former outstanding pitcher like Jerry Koosman manages just a 3-15 record, it's time to take stock. In other words, the end of the tailspin wasn't really in sight.

So it wasn't surprising when prior to the 1979 season Koosman was dealt to the Minnesota Twins for Greg Field and Jesse Orosco. Manager Joe Torre was saddled with another weak team that year, attendance fell to an all-time low of 788,905 fans and the club finished last once more in the NL East with a 63-99 record. Mazzilli led the club with a .303 average and tied newcomer Richie Hebner for the RBI lead with 79, while Joel Youngblood, not a slugger, led in homers with 16.

Craig Swan became the number one starter and finished with a 14-13 mark despite little support. But the most wins any other pitcher could muster was six. Pat Zachry was hurt most of the year and names like Kobel, Murray, Ellis, Hassler,

Opposite: *Hubie Brooks was another fine young player to join the New Yorkers in the 1980s. Hubie started out as a third baseman and is shown completing a force out during 1982 action.*

Below: *The old meets the new in this 1983 photo. Tom Seaver had returned to add stability to a young staff and young Ron Darling was just beginning his Mets career.*

Right: *In February 1982, the Mets signed longtime Cincinnati slugger George Foster to a 5 year, $10 million contract.*

Below: *Dave Kingman returned to the Mets in 1981 and showed he could still hit the long ball.*

Hausman, and Glynn were largely forgettable, a far cry from the Seaver-Koosman-Gentry-Matlack-McGraw years. The entire situation looked futile. After the season, Ed Kranepool, who had spent his entire 18-year career with the Mets, announced his retirement. He was the last link to the expansionist Mets of 1962, and his retirement symbolized the end of an era. Then, shortly after the season ended, the Payson family put the ball club up for sale.

The new ownership was a group headed by Doubleday & Company, the publishing giant. They took over the club on January 24, 1980, and less than a month later made a major move when they named Frank Cashen the new general manager. Cashen, who had been highly successful in the same capacity at Baltimore, would be looked upon as the main architect in the rebuilding scheme.

Changes in 1980 were less than sweeping. But there was a resurgence of attendance at Shea, not quite back to the glory years, but at least the people were returning. Maybe that was because the club hung in there until after the All-Star break. In fact, by August 2, they were just six and one-half games out of first and people were talking miracle once again. But suddenly the team slumped and slumped badly. They just didn't have the overall talent to hang in there.

They finished the year at 67-95, three games ahead of last place Chicago. Henderson hit .290, while Mazzilli was the top power man with 16 homers and 76 RBIs. The pitching, however, was lacking. Mark Bombeck led the staff with 10 wins, while Allen had 22 saves. Pat Zachry, acquired in the Seaver trade, continued to disappoint at 6-10. But attendance was back over the million mark, and that was a step in the right direction.

In 1981, some old faces returned. Dave Kingman and Rusty Staub rejoined the club, while rookies Hubie Brooks and Mookie Wilson began contributing at third and in centerfield. But the pitching was weak and there wasn't much power production aside from Kingman's 22 homers. It was the year of the strike and split season, so the club played just 102 games, finishing 41-62 on the year.

Then there were more changes. At season's end, it was announced that Joe Torre would not return as manager. In fairness to Torre, he was consistently saddled with bad clubs and had little chance to work with a winning team. The new manager was George Bamberger, who had done a fine job with the Milwaukee Brewers.

The team added more offense by acquiring former Cincinnati slugging star George Foster. He joined Kingman and Ellis Valentine (who had come over from Montreal late in 1981) to give the club a trio of potential sluggers. Lee Mazzilli was then traded to Texas for a pair of young pitching prospects, Ron Darling and Walt Terrell. Shortstop Ron Gardenhire and second sacker Wally Backman also became an in-

tegral part of the team. Though the pitching was weak, the look of the club was definitely changing.

At first, things looked good. The new Mets, or "Bambi's Bandits," as they were called, had a 34-30 record on June 20, and were just three games out of first place. But as had been the pattern in recent years, the second half was a disaster and the club wound up in familiar digs, the basement, with a 65-97 record. Craig Swan, with an 11-7 mark, was the only pitcher with double-digit victories and that was the major problem.

Offensively, there was a little more diversity. Kingman had 37 homers and 99 ribbies, but hit just .204. Foster smacked 13 homers and drove home 70 runs, not bad, but a far cry from his production with the Reds. Young Mookie Wilson set a club record with 58 steals. Catcher John Stearns hit .293, but Valentine was a disappointment in the power department, as was Hubie Brooks. There was obviously much more to be done, though attendance at Shea was back up to 1,320,055, the best since 1976.

Then came 1983, a year that would again mark a transition. The season would feature a touch of the old, a touch of class, and a touch of the new. And it would mark a new era in New York Mets baseball history.

Below: *George Bamberger (31) was the new Mets manager in 1982. Here Bambi greets the troops at the start of his first spring training with the New Yorkers.*

6. A Franchise Reborn

Below: *Sweet-swinging Danny Heep provided the Mets with a reliable bat off the bench in the mid-1980s. Heep could both fill in as an outfielder and pinch hit with equal success.*

For many Mets fans, the rebirth started on December 16, 1982. That was the day the team reacquired Tom Seaver. That's right, the man they called The Franchise for so long had returned after a six-year absence. Seaver would be 38 years old in 1983 and was coming off his poorest season ever, a 5-13 year in 1982. But just a season before, in strike shortened 1981, Tom Terrific was 14-2 and seemingly headed for another 20-game year.

No matter how he pitched, Seaver was perhaps the biggest symbol of the Mets' success. Just having him back where he

"belonged" seemed a step in the right direction. He gave the team a touch of the old.

Second baseman Brian Giles and shortstop José Oquendo also saw considerable action with the "new" Mets. Rusty Staub had become a pinch hitter extraordinaire, while Kingman was relegated to part-time status by injury and the inability to hit for a high average. Bob Bailor, Danny Heep, and Junior Ortiz gave the team added depth. Seaver was joined by veteran Mike Torrez, Swan, Ed Lynch, and Walt Terrell in the starting rotation, while Jesse Orosco and Doug Sisk were the main men out of the bullpen.

But there were two other players joining the Mets shortly after the 1983 season began. Each would have a major impact on the fortunes of the team over the next several years. The first came via a trade with the Cardinals on June 15. He was Keith Hernandez, a former National League batting champion, Most Valuable Player, and one of the finest fielding first basemen in baseball history.

Hernandez was just 29 years old when he joined the New Yorkers and quickly made his presence felt. He would show the young Mets how the game was supposed to be played and how to win. He definitely added a touch of class.

The other player joining the club in 1983 was one of the most heralded rookies to come along in years. He was a 6'6", 195 pound 21-year-old left-handed slugger named Darryl Strawberry. Strawberry had been the Mets number one draft choice and the top pick in the entire nation in June of 1980. He had been making his way through the minors and had completed a 34-home run, 97-RBI season with Jackson in Double A in 1982.

All spring, the team debated on what to do with Strawberry. Should he be kept in the majors or sent to Triple A for more seasoning? It was finally decided to send him down, but when the team got off to another terrible start, Strawberry was recalled the first week in May. And he soon brought the ball club something very new – a bona fide slugger with unlimited potential.

Left: *The acquisition of former batting king and MVP Keith Hernandez from St. Louis midway through the 1983 season is often considered a turning point for the Mets. Hernandez gave the club a clutch hitter, a leader, and a gold glove at first.*

Below: *Rookie outfielder Darryl Strawberry came up in May of 1983 with all kinds of advance notice. Though he struggled early, the Straw wound up with 26 homers and the Rookie of the Year Award.*

By early June, there was a sudden and unexpected change. Manager Bamberger resigned on June 3, and was replaced by coach Frank Howard, who also had previous managerial experience. Howard made a few lineup changes but decided to leave his struggling young slugger alone. Even though Strawberry was batting a paltry .161 on June 5, Howard left him in the lineup, and pretty soon the youngster began to hit.

Over the final 54 games of the year, Darryl hit .313 with 14 homers and 34 RBIs. He finished the year with a .257 average, 26 homers and 74 runs batted in. He would also become only the third Met (after Seaver and Matlack) to be named National League Rookie of the Year. It certainly looked as if the Mets had the makings of a superstar slugger, a commodity they always lacked.

Unfortunately, the rest of the Mets didn't finish as strongly as Darryl. It was another season in the NL East basement, the team finished at 68-94 for the year. Only this time, the finish was deceptive. There was more talent on the club than there had been for some time.

Strawberry, of course, looked to be a future super talent. Hernandez also didn't disappoint, hitting a solid .306 with 9 homers and 37 RBIs in just 320 at bats as a Met. And George Foster rebounded to lead the club with 28 homers and 90 ribbies in

Right: *This was a sight Mets fans would see often in the 1980s – Keith Hernandez coming through in the clutch.*

Below: *Davey Johnson took over as Mets manager in 1984 and the team promptly won 90 games.*

Bottom: *The 1984 Rookie of the Year pitcher, Dwight Gooden, won 17 games and led the league in strikeouts. And he was just 19 years old.*

his second year in New York. Hubie Brooks drove in 58 runs and speedy Mookie Wilson had 51 RBIs and 54 stolen bases. Kingman contributed 13 homers off the bench, while Danny Heep clubbed 8 in a reserve role.

The pitching still needed help. Tom Seaver wasn't the Tom Terrific of old. He pitched in tough luck while compiling a 9-14 record, but he was still good enough to win. Mike Torrez was 10-17, Ed Lynch 10-10 and young Walt Terrell 8-8. The top winner was reliever Jesse Orosco who was 13-7 in addition to 17 saves. To some, they may have seemed like the same old Mets with the same old problems. But more astute observers might have seen it coming. The club was getting closer and there was help just around the corner.

That corner would begin to turn right after the end of the 1983 season. Frank Howard, who was only the interim manager, was dismissed after the season ended and on October 13, Davey Johnson was named the new skipper.

Johnson had been a highly successful minor league manager, having piloted the Mets top farm team at Tidewater to the Triple A World Series in 1983. But that wasn't Johnson's only connection to the Mets. When the New Yorkers took their dramatic World Series win in 1969, Johnson was the Orioles' second baseman and the man who flied out to Cleon Jones to end the Series and make the Mets champions. Now he was going to try to make them champions again, only this time from the bench.

There was one front-office blunder before the new season began. The Mets once again lost the services of Tom Seaver. After only one year back at Shea, Seaver was lost to the Chicago White Sox because the Mets didn't protect him on their roster. Seaver would win 31 games in his first two years with the Sox, going over the 300-victory mark in a Hall of Fame career.

But the New Yorkers still had firepower. Hernandez, Foster, Strawberry, and Brooks gave the offense punch; Wilson, Wally Backman, and Strawberry gave it speed. And even with Seaver gone, the pitching staff had a young right-hander who become the talk of training camp. He was 19-year-old Dwight Gooden, who had a fastball reminiscent of Nolan Ryan's, a curve that broke off the table, and poise beyond his years.

Gooden was 19-4 at Lynchburg in A ball in 1983, and quickly showed he was ready for the jump to the majors. He was joined in the starting rotation by youngsters Ron Darling and Walt Terrell, steady Ed Lynch and eventually veteran Bruce Berenyi, who would come over from Cincinnati in a June trade. Hard-throwing young lefty, Sid Fernandez, would also contribute in the second half of the season.

With all the elements in place, the Mets quickly showed they were a completely different team than in the recent past. This team was a winner and looked as if it was just a few players short of being a true contender. As it was, the club was in the race for a good bit of the year. Though a number of players, such as Hernandez and Strawberry, put together solid years, and veteran Ray Knight helped stabilize the infield after an August trade, it was the hard-throwing Dwight Gooden who really made the headlines.

The youngster looked like instant Hall of Fame material. Whenever he pitched, he put extra people in the seats and he usually put on a show. He finished the year with a 17-9 record and 2.60 earned run average. What's more, he became the first teenager to lead the league in strikeouts. And his 276 K's established a rookie record, while his average of 11.39 strikeouts per nine inning game was a new major league mark. He quickly acquired the nickname of Dr. K, later shortened to The Doctor, then just Doc. It came as a surprise to no one when the young right-hander followed Strawberry as NL Rookie of the Year.

With Gooden leading the way, the Mets surprised everyone by finishing second in their division with a 90-72 record. It was the second best record in 23 years of franchise history and left the team just six and one-half games behind division winning Chicago. In addition, attendance was back up to 1,829,482, highest mark since 1973.

Following Gooden on the hill was Darling with 12 wins, Terrell with 11, Orosco with 10 and a club record 31 saves. The club finally had the makings of a real pitching staff once again. The hitting was also stronger. Hernandez led the club with a .311 mark, adding 15 homers and 94 RBIs. Strawberry hit 26 homers again, and drove home 97 runs, while Foster had 24 round-trippers and 86 RBIs. Hubie Brooks drove home 73 to go with 16 homers. Even Mookie Wilson slammed out 10 homers and added 54 ribbies. The Mets no longer played mediocre baseball; they had to be considered serious contenders in 1985.

In spite of their success in 1984, the team didn't rest on its laurels. GM Cashen and manager Johnson continued to improve the ball club and they did it in a big way. In December, the team made a trade with the Montreal Expos, acquiring All-Star catcher Gary Carter in exchange for Hubie Brooks, catcher Mike Fitzgerald and two minor leaguers. Carter was an outstanding defensive catcher who could handle the young

Left: *A meeting of the minds. Manager Davey Johnson and GM Frank Cashen discuss new ways for the Mets to win.*

Below: *Ed Lynch gave the Mets of the mid-1980s a strong right arm that could both start and relieve.*

Bottom: *Righty Bruce Berenyi came to the Mets from the Reds midway through 1984 and won 9 games.*

Right: *Catcher Gary Carter was already an all-star when he joined the Mets from Montreal in 1985. He added leadership and power to the club, as well as outstanding work behind the plate. Reliever Jesse Orosco had 31 saves in 1984 and was one of the best closers in the league.*

Opposite top left: *Dwight Gooden.*

Opposite top right: *Howard Johnson.*

Opposite bottom left: *Rick Aguilera.*

Opposite bottom right: *Roger McDowell.*

pitchers in addition to being one of the best RBI men in the league. It looked like a great deal.

There was also a trade with Detroit that brought in switch-hitting third baseman Howard Johnson in exchange for pitcher Terrell. Rafael Santana took over at shortstop, scrappy Len Dykstra began seeing time in the outfield, while pitchers Roger McDowell and Rick Aguilera also began contributing. So the team was deeper and more balanced than it had ever been before. Barring some key injuries, the 1985 Mets were expected to have a fine year.

They didn't disappoint. In fact, most of the players they depended on came through. And no one had a bigger year than 20-year-old Dwight Gooden. The Doctor took up where he left off as a rookie, then elevated his game another notch or two. Without a doubt, he was baseball's best pitcher in 1985 and he led a charge that saw the new Mets battle the St. Louis Cardinals right down to the wire. And they did it despite losing Darryl Strawberry for seven weeks with an injured thumb.

Playing hard to the end, the Mets wound up with a 98-64 record and weren't eliminated until the second-to-last day of the season. Only a splendid, 101-61 record by St. Louis prevented the Mets from taking the divisional crown. For a team that had been a basement ball club until two seasons ago, it was a glorious return, one which had begun the year before.

Dwight Gooden was the talk of baseball. The Doctor finished the year with an amazing, 24-4 record. He would become the youngest Cy Young Award winner and youngest 20-game winner in baseball history. Among other things, he set a club record with an incredible 1.53 earned run average and fanned a major league best 268 hitters. But the Doc wasn't the only arm in town. He had help from young Ron Darling who produced a fine, 16-6, season. Ed Lynch and Rick Aguilera won 10 games each, while Roger McDowell and Jesse Orosco had 17 saves apiece and won 14 games between them.

Gary Carter, in his first Mets season, didn't disappoint. The "Kid" had a solid .281 average to go with a club leading 32 home runs and 100 RBIs. Hernandez was also outstanding. He took his eighth straight Gold Glove Award at first, had 24 game-winning RBIs, a tribute to his clutch hitting, and batted .309 with 10 homers and 91 ribbies. Despite missing seven weeks, Strawberry chipped in with 29 dingers and 79 RBIs. The aging George Foster was still good enough to slam 21 balls into the seats and drive home 77 runs.

And there was plenty of help from the role players, as well. No doubt about it, these Mets were a team. In fact, the season had been undeniably great with one exception. The team fell three games short. So as 1986 approached, the Mets still had something to prove.

7. A Season to Remember

For the first time in their history, the New York Mets were installed as favorites in the National League East before the 1986 season began. In addition, there were many observers who felt the New Yorkers were not only the best in their division, but the best overall team in all of baseball.

And it would be hard to argue. A trade with the Boston Red Sox brought left-hander Bob Ojeda to the ball club. He would join Gooden, Darling, Fernandez, and Aguilera to form a potentially outstanding starting rotation. Utility infielder Tim Teufel also helped add depth, and a scrappy rookie named Kevin Mitchell hit so well in spring training that he forced the club to keep him in the big leagues.

This time, the Mets didn't fool around. They moved into first place on April 23, and that was it. No divisional race. No down-to-the-wire finishes. The team simply lived up to expectations, played up to its potential, and made a shambles of the National League East. The only question was how many games they would finish in front and how they would perform once the playoffs rolled around.

The Mets had assembled a truly fine baseball team. Carter and Hernandez were both All-Stars, and the deals that brought them to New York were among the team's best. Along with Ray Knight, these veterans knew how to win and managed to impart their knowledge to the younger players. It was the kind of blend that makes up most championship teams. There was outstanding pitching, good power, and good speed. All the ingredients were there in abundance. And when the team stayed relatively free of injury, that did it.

By the All-Star break the club had broken the race wide open. Shea Stadium was a rocking, fun place to be as 2,762,417 fans would cheer for the Mets, a team that in its silver anniversary season had become overpowering. When the ball club stretched its lead to 22 full games on September 10, that represented the biggest lead of any team in the history of divisional play,

Right: *Pitching coach Mel Stottlemyre (l) talks with 4 of his 1986 starters: (l to r) Stottlemyre, Bob Ojeda, Sid Fernandez, Ron Darling, and Dwight Gooden. By this time, it was generally agreed that the Mets had the best staff in baseball.*

which began in 1969. The title clincher came against the Cubs seven days later, a 4-2 victory that gave the New Yorkers the earliest calendar clinching in National League East history.

The team rolled to 108 victories, obviously a club record. In fact, the Mets were just the ninth team in modern baseball history to win that many ballgames. They also set club records for home runs with 148, team batting average at .263, and attendance. And the individual performances were just as impressive.

Second baseman Wally Backman hit .320 in 387 at bats, while Hernandez led the regulars at .310. Keith also won his 9 straight Gold Glove, smacked 13 homers and drove home 83 runs. Carter tied a team record with 105 RBIs to go along with his 24 homers. Strawberry smacked 27 homers and drove in 93 runs, while Knight had 11 round-trippers and 76 RBIs to go with a .298 average. But there were solid contributions right down the line.

On the mound, Gooden wasn't quite as dominating as he had been in 1985. But the Doctor was still 17-6 with a 2.84 ERA and 200 strikeouts. Bob Ojeda, who had come over from the Red Sox, mesmerized National League hitters with his fine assortment of curves and off-speed pitches and finished at 18-5. Darling was 15-6, Sid Fernandez 16-6 with 200 strikeouts, while Aguilera finished at 10-7. All the starters were winners, a far cry from the early days of the franchise.

Even the bullpen was outstanding. Roger McDowell set a club mark with 75 appearances and had 22 saves to go with a 14-9 record. And Jesse Orosco saved 21 while compiling an 8-6 mark and 2.33 ERA. But no team can rest on its laurels for long. The playoffs were fast approaching and they

Top left: *The heart of the Mets lineup, Gary Carter, Darryl Strawberry, and Keith Hernandez get together during spring training in 1985.*

Left: *Former Minnesota Twin Tim Teufel provided the Mets with a solid glove and strong right-handed bat after joining the team in 1986.*

Below: *Rookie Kevin Mitchell hit so well in spring training of 1986 that the Mets kept him with the big club all year.*

Above: *Bob Ojeda, the crafty lefthander who came to the Mets from Boston in 1986, baffled National League hitters to the tune of an 18-5 record.*

were now a best of seven series instead of the best of five from earlier days. And the Mets would be meeting a team that was always tough for them, the Houston Astros.

In 1986, the Astros won 96 to take the NL West by 10 games. In the eyes of most, Houston wasn't nearly as balanced or deep as the Mets. But they had some solid pitching and the ability to be a kind of scrappy, pesky team. But out of all those elements, it was the Houston pitching that the Mets feared most.

Veteran strikeout king and former Met Nolan Ryan was still a formidable opponent at 39, while lefties Bob Knepper and Jim Deshaies always seemed to pitch well against the Mets. But the man the New Yorkers really feared was hard-throwing right-hander Mike Scott, who had originally come up with the Mets in 1979. Traded to Houston in 1983, Scott emerged as an 18-8 hurler in 1985, and a year later became a dominating mound presence. He was 18-10 on the year, led the league with a 2.22 earned run average and 306 strikeouts. His efforts would result in a Cy Young Award after the season. Scott said the split-fingered fastball turned his career around. But others accused him of doing tricks with the ball. "Scotty the Scuffer" was a nickname given him by opponents.

The opener, played in the Houston Astrodome, was a classic confrontation between two great pitchers, Gooden and Scott. After a scoreless first, Houston's cleanup hitter Glenn Davis led off the second and blasted a long home run to centerfield to make it 1-0.

No one knew it then, but Davis's homer would be the only run of the game. Scott was nothing short of brilliant. He struck out 14 Mets while scattering 5 hits. Both teams played outstanding defense to stifle several potential rallies. When it ended, Houston had a 1-0 victory, a 1-0 lead in the series, and Mike Scott had definitely sent a message to his former teammates. Now the Mets faced their first "must" game of the post-season in the second contest.

This time it was lefty Bob Ojeda against the other former Met, Nolan Ryan. The game was scoreless for three innings before the New Yorkers broke it open. They scored two in the fourth and three more in the fifth to drive Ryan from the mound. Ojeda, meanwhile, scattered 10 hits and held the Astros to a single run in the seventh. The 5-1 victory tied the series and sent both teams flying back to New York for game three.

Ron Darling and Bob Knepper were the opposing pitchers, and when the Astros got a pair in the first and two more in the second for a 4-0 lead, things began looking bleak because Mike Scott was poised to start the next day. The 4-0 score stood until the bottom of the sixth when the New Yorkers finally got to the crafty left-hander. A three-run homer by Strawberry keyed a four-run rally to tie the game.

The deadlock didn't last long. In the top half of the seventh the Astros built a run against Rick Aguilera and took a 5-4 lead. It still stood that way when the Mets came up for their final at bat facing Houston closer Dave Smith. With Scott waiting in the wings for game four, the New Yorkers' backs were clearly up against the wall.

Scrappy Wally Backman led off and promptly drilled a single. He then took second on a pass ball before pinch hitter Danny Heep flied to center for the first out. Now leadoff hitter Lenny Dykstra was up. The man they call "Nails" wasn't known as a long ball threat, but he got the pitch he wanted and hit a long drive to deep right-field. The ball was gone! The Mets had won it on a dramatic, last-minute home run by an unlikely hero. They now had a 2-1 lead in the series and braced themselves to face Mike Scott again.

Scott was going on just three days rest, so manager Davey Johnson decided to send Sid Fernandez up against Houston, giving Dwight Gooden the extra day to be ready for game five. Maybe it was a good thing, because Mike Scott was on his game once more and the Mets looked futile against him. Scott topped the Mets again, 3-1, in another superb performance. The series was tied at two games each and what was to follow were a pair of the most exciting contests in Mets annals.

Game five, the last at Shea before a return to Houston, pitted Dwight Gooden against Nolan Ryan. To some, it was a battle between the king and the heir apparent. Ryan took up the challenge, turned back the clock, and began pitching a brilliant baseball game. In fact, the hard-throwing veteran all but outpitched the younger Gooden. A Strawberry home run gave the Mets a run in the fifth after Houston pushed one across in the top of the inning. And that was the only scoring the two fireballers allowed for nine innings.

Ryan was especially stingy, giving up two hits while striking out 12. He didn't tire at all, retiring the final seven Mets he faced after walking Strawberry in the seventh. Gooden was nearly as good and the game went into extra innings. Charlie Kerfeld replaced Ryan in the tenth and Orosco came on for Gooden to start the eleventh. But it was in the twelfth that the game ended.

That's when Wally Backman ignited things again with an infield hit. He went to second when a Kerfeld pickoff throw went awry. Then Keith Hernandez was walked intentionally to set up the double-play possibility and bring up Gary Carter, who had hit just 1 for 21 in the playoffs. But the veteran came through, slamming a base hit to drive in the winning run. Now the Mets returned to the Astrodome with a 3-2 lead and hoping to wrap things up in game six.

Despite the one-game cushion, the Mets wanted game six badly. Many felt the entire team was wary about the prospect of having to face Mike Scott a third time if the series went to seven games. And that made number six even more dramatic as Bob Ojeda took to the hill against Bob Knepper. And it was the Astros who struck first. Four first-inning hits against Ojeda gave Houston three runs.

Even though Ojeda settled down after the first, Knepper kept putting the Mets aside with some nifty pitching. By the time the New Yorkers came to bat in the ninth inning, they found themselves trailing by that same, 3-0, margin. Once again, the widely acknowledged best team in baseball had its back up against the wall.

Pinch hitter Lenny Dykstra opened the inning with a clutch triple to deep center-field. Then Mookie Wilson slapped a single and Dykstra scored the first Met run. After a ground out which sent Wilson to second, Hernandez lashed a clutch double to score

Mookie with the second run. Dave Smith then replaced Knepper and walked both Carter and Strawberry. Ray Knight was next and his long fly to right center scored the tying run.

From there the game went into extra innings and became an epic battle. Neither team could score for the next four innings. Then, in the top of the fourteenth the Mets broke through. Backman drove in the run with a clutch hit, but in the bottom of the inning, Billy Hatcher slammed a home run off McDowell to tie the game once again.

Now the two teams moved into the sixteenth. Then the Mets struck again. This time Strawberry blooped a double to center and scored on a single by Knight. That made it 5-4. A wild pitch and single by Dykstra got two more home and before the inning ended, the Mets were on top, 7-4, and three outs away from a pennant.

But the Astros didn't go quietly. Facing Jesse Orosco, Houston rallied again, scoring twice and pulling to 7-6. Then, with the tying run in scoring position, Orosco reached back and struck out Kevin Bass to end the game and the playoffs. The Mets were once again National League champions. Now, there was just one more hurdle to clear.

Standing in the way were the Boston Red

Below: *Lefty Sid Fernandez emerged as a star in 1986 when he compiled a 16-6 record with 200 strikeouts.*

Bottom: *Scrappy second baseman Wally Backman was an ignitor who always got his uniform dirty. His grit and determination started one rally after another.*

Right: *Mookie Wilson continued to give the Mets speed on the basepaths throughout the 1980s.*

Below: *Darryl Strawberry showed his power by winning the home run hitting contest before the 1986 All-Star Game. When the Straw was on one of his hot streaks he was capable of carrying the whole team.*

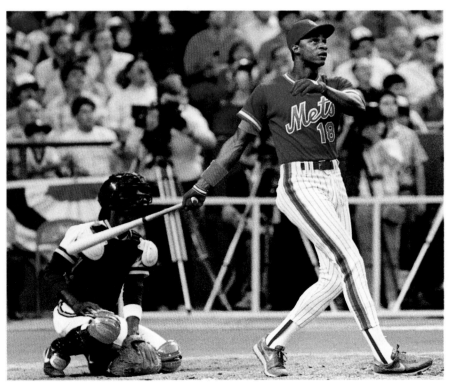

Sox. The BoSox had taken the American League East by five and one-half games over the Yankees, then defeated the California Angels in the playoffs. During that series, the Sox trailed three games to one, and at one point were just a strike away from elimination when Dave Henderson hit a dramatic, two-run homer to keep them in it. They then romped past the Angels in the seventh game, 8-1, behind their ace, Roger Clemens, to join the Mets in the Series.

Clemens had duplicated what Dwight Gooden had done in 1985, compiling a 24-4 record during the regular season. He had solid help from Dennis "Oil Can" Boyd and Bruce Hurst, giving the BoSox a Big Three. Former Met Tom Seaver, in his final season, contributed five wins to the Sox pennant push before a leg injury put him on the shelf.

The Sox also had plenty of sock. Jim Rice and Bill Buckner each topped the 100 RBI mark, while Dwight Evans had 97 and Don Baylor 94. Those four also had 95 homers between them. They also had American League batting champ Wade Boggs, who hit .357. The two things that made the Mets favorites were relief pitching and team speed. The Sox were slow.

Ron Darling and Bruce Hurst were the opening game pitchers as 55,076 fans rocked Shea Stadium to the rafters. They expected hitting, but instead they got pitching. The two starters were both sharp and threw nothing but goose-eggs for the first six innings. Then in the top of the seventh, the Sox scored a run on a Tim Teufel error. It proved to be the only run of the game. The Mets managed just four singles off Hurst. Calvin Schiraldi worked the ninth for the save.

Down one game, the Mets sent their ace, Dwight Gooden, after the Sox in game two. The Doctor would be opposed by the Rocket, Roger Clemens. These were the guys who were expected to put on the pitching duel and guess what? They didn't!

Nothing happened for the first two frames, but in the third Boston jumped on top with three runs off the Doctor. Then in the bottom of the inning, the Mets got two back. But the Sox would get another in the fourth, two more in the fifth, a pair in the seventh and one more in the ninth to win easily, 9-3. Gooden lasted only five innings and was tagged for six runs, while Clemens was yanked after just four and one-third frames, and the Sox bullpen surprised everyone by holding down the New Yorkers.

Suddenly, the Mets were in big trouble. Not only did they trail, 2-0, in the Series, a deficit few teams have made up in a seven-game series, but they had also lost both

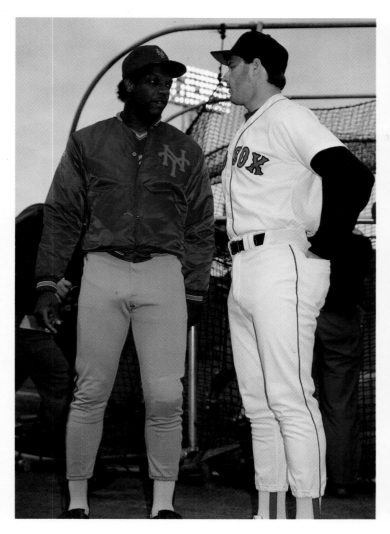

games at home. Now they would be playing the next three (if three were needed) in the Red Sox backyard that was cozy Fenway Park. And that was a place where visitors had a tough time winning.

So the pressure was really on when Bob Ojeda took to the mound against his former teammates. He was opposed by Oil Can Boyd. As they had done all year when their backs were up against the wall, the Mets made a statement.

Lenny Dykstra led off and nailed the third pitch of the game just inside the right-field foul pole for a home run. In the same inning Carter doubled home Wally Backman and Danny Heep singled home Carter and Hernandez. Before the 33, 595 fans at Fenway had settled into their seats, the Mets had a 4-0 lead.

That would be all Bob Ojeda needed. The former BoSox handcuffed his old teammates, holding them to five hits and one run in seven innings. Roger McDowell hurled the final two frames as the Mets won it, 7-1, pounding out 13 hits in the process. The New Yorkers were back in it, but they still had to win the pivotal fourth game. Otherwise, they would trail, 3-1, and still have a long road to travel.

The Mets went back to opening-game starter Ron Darling, but the Red Sox decided to give their pitchers an extra day's rest and called on their number four starter, Al Nipper. It was a risk that didn't pay off. The Mets got to Nipper in the fourth inning on a two-run homer by Carter and run-scoring single by Knight. They got two more in the seventh and another in the top of the eighth to take a 6-0 lead. The final was 6-2 and the Mets had evened the Series at two games each.

Now it was Gooden's turn again, but this time he would be going up against a well-rested Bruce Hurst. There was trouble from the beginning. The Doctor just wasn't sharp. The Sox touched him for a run in the second and another in the third. And when they got another pair in the fifth before anyone was retired, Gooden was removed in favor of Sid Fernandez. It didn't matter that El Sid pitched four shutout innings because the damage had already been done.

Hurst cruised home with a 4-2 victory, his second win of the Series. More importantly, it enabled the BoSox to move ahead once again, this time by a 3-2 count. Now the teams would return to Shea for game six. And worst yet, the Mets would be facing the best pitcher in baseball during 1986, Roger Clemens.

Above left: *The Mets' Dwight Gooden and the Red Sox Roger Clemens talk shop before the 1986 World Series. The "Doctor" had the best record in baseball in 1985 and the "Rocket" took that honor in 1986.*

Above right: *Jesse Orosco continued to work his relief magic throughout the 1986 playoffs and World Series. The lefty stopper appeared in 8 of 13 post-season games.*

Bob Ojeda was given the unenvious job of opposing Clemens and trying to keep his team from extinction. It wouldn't be easy to begin with and it got more difficult quickly, because the Sox scored single runs in the first and second to jump on top, 2-0. With five days rest, that might be all the Rocket Man needed.

In the early innings Clemens indeed looked sharp. Fortunately, Ojeda also settled down and the 2-0 margin remained until the bottom of the fifth. The Mets didn't have a base hit to that time, but got it started when Strawberry drew a walk. Darryl then stole second and scored on a clutch base hit by Ray Knight. When Mookie Wilson singled to right, Knight went all the way to third as rightfielder Dwight Evans bobbled the ball. It was an important play, because pinch hitter Danny Heep then hit into a double play that allowed Knight to come home with the tying run.

The score remained knotted until the top of the seventh. Roger McDowell had taken over from Ojeda. A walk, groundout, throwing error, and force play gave the Sox the go-ahead run. With a 3-2 lead, the Red Sox were now nine outs away from being world champions.

Clemens left the game after seven and as the Mets came up in the eighth they were facing reliever Calvin Schiraldi. Lee Mazzilli, who had returned to the team as a pinch hitter for the final 39 games of 1986, led off the eighth with a single. He was then sacrificed to second by Dykstra, who beat the throw to first on a fielder's choice. A sacrifice by Backman moved both runners up and then Hernandez was walked intentionally to load the bases.

Carter then stepped in and drove home Mazzilli with a sacrifice fly to left. That's all Mets got, but the game was tied again. The big crowd at Shea was on the edge of their seats as neither team scored in the ninth and the game went into the tenth inning. Rick Aguilera, who had retired the Sox in the ninth, ran into trouble in the first extra frame.

Boston touched the righty for three hits and two runs, one of them coming in on a homer by Dave Henderson. When Aguilera finally retired the side, the Shea Stadium crowd was almost silent. Boston's two runs

Opposite top: *Lenny Dykstra (r) lived up to his nickname of "Nails" when he belted a leadoff homer for the Mets in game three of the 1986 World Series.*

Opposite bottom left: *Third baseman Ray Knight batted .391 for the Series and ignited the Mets with his fierce competitive spirit.*

Opposite bottom right: *Lee Mazzilli starred with the Mets during the lean years of the late 1970s. In 1986 he returned to the team and became a top pinch hitter.*

Below left: *Dwight Gooden in action. The Doctor operating during the 1986 World Series.*

Right: *Shortstop Rafael Santana was a steadying force in the Mets infield for several years beginning in 1985.*

Opposite top: *The Mets Gary Carter comes sliding home against Red Sox catching counterpart Rich Gedman during the 1986 Series.*

Opposite bottom: *Boston's Wade Boggs tries to run down the Mets' Mookie Wilson during the battle for the world title in 1986.*

gave them a 5-3 lead. But what was on everyone's mind was the fact that the Mets were now just three outs away from losing the World Series.

Schiraldi was still pitching for the BoSox and he promptly retired the first two Mets on routine outfield flies. As Gary Carter stepped in, the New Yorkers were down to their final out. Carter would say later that all that kept going through his mind was that he didn't want to make the final out of the Series. He concentrated, fought off Schiraldi, and then with two strikes on him rapped a single to left.

Rookie Kevin Mitchell then stepped up as a pinch hitter. What a spot for a first-year player. Mitchell singled to center, sending Carter to second. The Mets weren't done yet. Ray Knight was next. Still trying to atone for his seventh-inning error, Knight smacked a base hit to center which scored Carter and sent Mitchell to third. Schiraldi was then removed in favor of veteran Bob Stanley as Mookie Wilson stepped up.

Stanley promptly threw a wild pitch, which the acrobatic Wilson jumped and twisted to avoid, and Mitchell sprinted home with the tying run as the fans went wild. Wilson stepped back in, and finally hit a slow dribbler toward first. Bill Buckner came over to field it, bent down, then watched it go right through his legs. As Mookie flashed across the bag, Ray Knight sped home with the winning run!

The Mets had done it, made an amazing

comeback to win the sixth game, 6-5, and tie the Series once more. Now they really had something to shoot for. Only two teams in baseball history, the 1912 Red Sox and 1985 Royals had ever come back to win after being three outs away from elimination. Mercifully, there was a rainout the next day that allowed the teams to recover from the emotionally exhausting ball game.

The Red Sox went back to Bruce Hurst, who had pitched so well in the Series, and the Mets countered with Ron Darling, who had been their best. Everybody else was in the bullpen, because there was no tomorrow.

After a scoreless first, the Red Sox struck for three runs in the second frame. Fortunately, Darling settled down and pitched into the fourth until he was lifted in favor of Sid Fernandez. But as the Mets came up in the last of the sixth inning, they still trailed by that same 3-0 margin. Bruce Hurst was handling them again.

After Hurst got Rafael Santana to ground to short, Lee Mazzilli pinch-hit for Fernandez and singled. Mookie Wilson followed with another base hit and Tim Teufel walked to load the bases. Up stepped Keith Hernandez and as he had done all year, he came through, smacking a single to center that scored two runs. And when Carter bounced into a fielder's choice force play, the third run of the inning crossed home plate. The game was tied.

Roger McDowell took over in the seventh and quickly retired the BoSox. Then the Mets began to put the icing on the cake. With Calvin Schiraldi pitching, Ray Knight broke the tie by blasting a dramatic home run to centerfield. Pinch hitter Len Dykstra followed with a single and took second on a wild pitch. A single by Santana scored Dykstra to make it 5-3. And a sac fly by Hernandez gave the Mets their third run of the inning and a 6-3 lead.

The Sox made it interesting in the eighth when a pair of singles and an Evans double scored two runs and drove McDowell from the mound. Jesse Orosco came on to get the side out, but it was now a 6-5 game. Two insurance runs, one coming on a Strawberry homer, made the score 8-5 in the top of the ninth. Now the Mets were three outs away. And Jesse Orosco did the final job, shutting down the BoSox in the ninth inning and making the New York Mets world champions once more.

Ray Knight was named the Most Valuable Player in the Series, but in truth it had been a team effort, just as it had been all year. The Mets were deserving champions. They had a well-balanced, deep team, one that National League rivals knew they would have to fear for years to come.

8. A Question of Dynasty

There was a big difference between the Mets championship team of 1969 and the ball club that took it all in 1986. In 1969, the club was led by a superb pitching staff, anchored by two real aces. But the everyday players just caught fire and rode the flames to a title.

The 1986 team also had a superior mound corps. But this ball club was solid and balanced from top to bottom, with a blend of veterans and youngsters, the kind of team that should continue to win. And that's what everyone expected. When 1987 rolled around the Mets were still considered the team to beat.

There weren't too many changes in personnel, but there were some significant moves. At first glance, they seemed to strengthen the team. In December, the club traded hard-hitting Kevin Mitchell, along with two prospects, to San Diego in return for outfielder Kevin McReynolds. McReynolds was a power hitter and outstanding all-around player who was coming off a .288, 26-homer, 96-RBI season with the Padres. He was just 27 years old and the ball club felt it was getting an everyday leftfielder and potential superstar.

The club also picked up right-handed pitcher David Cone in a deal with the Kansas City Royals for backup catcher Ed Hearn, added infielder Dave Magadan, catcher Barry Lyons, and reliever Randy Myers. On paper, the Mets looked extremely strong.

There was one important deletion, however. The team could not agree on a new contract with Ray Knight, the World Series MVP. He ended up signing with Baltimore. While Howard Johnson took over at third and had an outstanding year, Knight's leadership abilities and mental toughness would be missed.

Yet had things gone smoothly from the first, chances are the Mets would have repeated their National League East triumph and gone on from there. But there were problems from the outset. For openers, Dwight Gooden would miss the first two months of the season while completing a substance-abuse rehabilitation program. That was the start of a season that would see Mets pitchers spend a total of 457 days on the disabled list. So despite some outstanding offensive contributions by a number of players, the ball club wound up finishing second to the St. Louis Cardinals, losing the divisional title by a scant three games.

Despite the injuries, their 92-70 record

Below: *The Mets work out at their new spring training site at Port St. Lucie, Florida, in February 1988.*

was the fourth best mark in club history and fourth best in the majors for 1987. So a case can be made for the pitching injuries keeping the ball club from repeating. Gooden didn't make his first start until June 5, yet still wound up with a 15-7 mark. Ron Darling and Sid Fernandez were both at 12-8, while Rick Aguilera was 11-3 and swing man Terry Leach 11-1 after winning his first 10 decisions. McDowell had 25 saves, Orosco 16. But Bob Ojeda, who won 18 the year before, spent almost the entire season on the disabled list and won just 3 games.

On the offensive side, the team simply hit a ton. The two great veterans, Hernandez and Carter, were again solid, but it was the youngsters who really shined. Strawberry broke the club record with 39 homers, hit .284, drove home 104 runs and swiped 36 bases. Third baseman Howard Johnson, now playing regularly, had 36 homers, 99 ribbies and 32 steals. Johnson and Strawberry became the first teammates in baseball history to hit more than 30 homers and steal more than 30 bases in the same season.

Newcomer McReynolds chipped in with 29 dingers and 95 runs batted in. Tim Teufel had 14 homers and 61 ribbies, while the centerfield platoon of Len Dykstra and Mookie Wilson together had 19 home runs. A far cry from the days when the Mets lacked even a single power hitter. And for the first time, attendance topped the 3 million mark at 3,027,121. So despite finishing second, the ball club was still exciting and made the immediate favorite for 1988.

As usual, there were a few roster changes. Jesse Orosco was gone, as was Rafael Santana. Randy Myers would become the number one closer and young Kevin Elster took over at short. Mackey Sasser joined the team as a third catcher and pinch lefty swinger. But basically it was the same team and they started the season quickly.

By the end of April the club was 15-6 and just a half game out of first. When Dwight Gooden threw his fourth consecutive complete game, shutting out the Reds, 11-0, on May 1, all seemed right with the Mets' world. In fact, the team seemed as powerful as ever.

Sure enough, on May 3, the Mets went into first place, and by the end of the month they were 34-15 and in front by four and one-half games. They were also getting an unexpectedly strong performance from right-hander David Cone. In the rotation for the first time, Cone was off to a 7-0 start and pitching as well as anyone in the National League.

The team's pace slowed a bit in June.

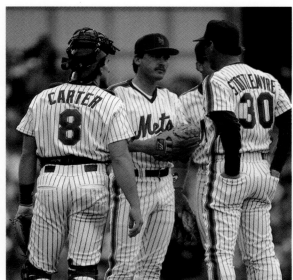

Above: *Outfielder Kevin McReynolds joined the Mets from San Diego in 1987. An all-around fine player, McReynolds had 29 homers and 95 RBIs in his first year as a New Yorker.*

Left: *Lefty reliever Randy Myers (c) confers with catcher Gary Carter (8) and pitching coach Mel Stottlemyre (30). The fastballer Myers became the Mets stopper out of the pen in 1988.*

Below left: *Righthander Rick Aguilera joined the Mets in 1985 and produced several fine seasons.*

Hernandez pulled a hamstring running the bases June 6, and had to go on the disabled list for the first time in his career. He wouldn't be back for two months. The club was just 15-13 in June, 14-12 in July and 15-14 in August. But with a little over a month to go, they still had a 78-54 record and a seven and one-half game lead in the division.

Then, in the final month, they picked up the pace again. The Mets were 20-6 during September, and won their only two games in October to finish the season with 100 victories against the 60 losses. They won the division by 15 games and set yet another Shea Stadium attendance record as 3,047,724 fans made their way through the turnstiles.

Some things didn't change. The pitchers stayed healthy and were outstanding. Cone had a super year, compiling a 20-3 record with 2.22 earned run average and 213 strikeouts. Gooden showed he was mortal, but still finished at 18-9. Darling was right behind at 17-9, while Fernandez was 12-10. McDowell had 16 saves and Myers 26 to go with a 1.72 earned run average.

Strawberry had another big year with 39 more homers and 101 ribbies, while McReynolds chipped in with 27 homers and 99 RBIs. Johnson had 24 round-trippers and drove home 68 runs, but his production was down from 1987. One bright spot was the late season emergence of highly touted rookie Gregg Jefferies. The young switch-hitter played in 29 games at the end of the season and hit .321, getting 35 hits, 6 homers and 17 ribbies. He was quickly touted as a phenom, a future batting champ, who had to have a place in the starting lineup.

Even though the club won 100 games, there was a change in the team balance. It could be found in the decreasing productivity of the two great veterans, Hernandez and Carter. Keith spent two months on the disabled list and wound up with a .276 average with 11 homers and 55 RBIs in 95 games. Carter, showing the wear and tear of all that catching, hit just .242 with 11 homers and 46 ribbies in 129 games. But the overall team still seemed to have more than any other ball club except maybe the American League Oakland A's. Mets fans hoped to see their heroes go up against sluggers José Canseco, Mark McGuire, and the rest of the A's in the World Series. But first the team had to win in the playoffs. They were heavy favorites against a team that wasn't even supposed to be there, the Los Angeles Dodgers.

The Dodgers were the surprise winners in the West, coming off two straight losing seasons to take division honors with a 94-67 record. The team wasn't especially deep, but they had a new field leader in slugger Kirk Gibson and a pitching superstar in Orel Hershiser. The often-injured Gibson finished the year with 25 homers and 76 RBIs, but his leadership qualities along with his clutch play would earn him the National League's Most Valuable Player Award. Hershiser came through with a 23-8 record and finished the season by setting a major league mark of 59 consecutive scoreless innings. The smooth-throwing right-hander would be the National League's Cy Young Award winner.

But Gibson, Hershiser, and company didn't seem to have enough overall firepower to whip the Mets. It was Hershiser and Gooden in the first game at Dodger Stadium in Los Angeles. At first it looked as if the Dodger right-hander was going to take up just where he left off in the regular season. He held a 2-0 lead after eight innings when he left the game. But the Mets jumped all over the Dodger relievers. Strawberry drove in the first run with a double. Then Carter smacked a two-out double and two more runs scampered home. When Randy Myers shut the Dodgers down in the ninth, the Mets had won the game, 3-2, coming through in the clutch just as they had back in 1986.

If the Mets could take the second game at L.A. the Dodgers would really be in trouble. They sent David Cone to face Tim Belcher. But Cone, who lost only three times during the regular season, didn't have it. The Dodgers touched him for five runs in the first two innings to put the game out of reach. Hernandez drove in three runs for the Mets, but the 6-3 final enabled the Dodgers to tie the series at a game each.

The two teams then returned to Shea Stadium for the third contest. It was a miserable night, with temperatures in the mid-30s and a cold drizzle falling. Once again, the Mets showed their ability to come from behind. Trailing in the eighth inning, they got a two-out, RBI double by Backman, a run-scoring single by Wilson, a bases loaded walk to Hernandez and two-run single by Strawberry to give them five runs and key an 8-4 victory.

With a 2-1 lead in games, the Mets again seemed in the driver's seat. Game four was the one in which the Mets could have probably put it away. And they almost did. Only this time it was the Dodgers who provided the eleventh-hour lightning. With Dwight Gooden on the hill, the New Yorkers were confident. But it took back-to-back homers

Below: *David Cone came to the Mets in a 1987 trade with Kansas City. A year later, the hard-throwing right-hander produced a sensational 20-3 record that helped his team to another NL East title.*

Above: *Twenty-one-year-old Gregg Jefferies played 29 games for the 1988 Mets, hitting .321 with 6 homers. He was touted as a phenom, a future star.*

by Strawberry and McReynolds in the fourth inning to give the Mets a 3-2 lead. By the ninth inning it was a 4-2 ball game with Gooden trying to wrap it up.

It never happened. Dodger catcher Mike Scioscia slammed a two-run game-tying homer off the Doctor and it went to extra innings. In the top of the twelfth, Gibson showed why he was the MVP. He blasted a

clutch home run off Roger McDowell to give the Dodgers a 5-4 lead. And when the Mets threatened in the bottom of the inning, Orel Hershiser made a surprise appearance out of the bullpen and got McReynolds to fly out to center, ending the ball game. The Dodgers had tied the series.

In the pivotal fifth game, the Mets ran into trouble again. This time the Dodgers

David Cone took to the mound in the sixth game and avenged his defeat in game two. He scattered five hits to win easily, 5-1. Kevin McReynolds was the hitting star and the series was tied once again. Now all came down to a single game. Ron Darling started it for the Mets, but the Dodgers were ready with their ace, Orel Hershiser.

Surprisingly, it was the Mets who cracked early. The Dodgers broke on top with five, second-inning runs as the New York defense fell apart. Jefferies made an error, Steve Sax smacked a two-run single, Backman made an error and John Shelby hit a sacrifice fly. That was all she wrote. Orel Hershiser showed why he was baseball's best pitcher in 1988. Despite a heavy workload at the end of the season and in the playoffs, he blanked the Mets on just five hits as the Dodgers won it, 6-0.

Mets players and fans were stunned. Now there would be no showdown with the Oakland A's. The Dodgers were National League champs and the Mets were going home. They had finally run out of miracle finishes. The team could only take up the Dodgers old cry from back in Brooklyn days.

Wait till next year!

Below: *Len Dykstra is greeted at home plate after belting a home run in game five of the 1988 playoffs against the Dodgers.*

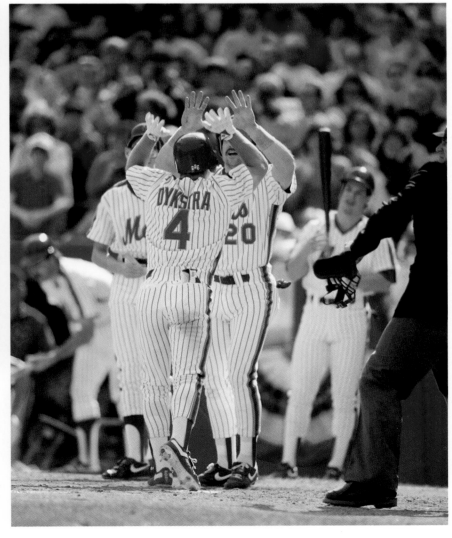

scored three runs in the fourth and three more in the fifth on a Gibson homer to take a 6-0 lead. That was enough for rookie right-hander Tim Belcher. The Dodgers won it, 7-4, and now had a 3-2 lead in the series. And game six would be back home for them at Dodger Stadium. The Mets would really need some kind of miracle to win it now.

Next year would again be a Mets year, most fans figured. After all, any team can falter in a short series, but the Mets were still one of the best two teams in baseball. There was pitching galore, plenty of power, good speed, great veterans, and a phenom in Gregg Jefferies. The team had also made manager Davey Johnson the first skipper in big league history to win 90 or more games in his first five full seasons.

But to the more astute observer, there was more than a subtle change to the overall makeup of the team, more internal bickering, fewer contented players and less fire in belly of the ball club. There didn't seem to be that burning desire to win, that one-for-all, all-for-one quality that characterized the team in 1986. And though some hated to admit it, Hernandez and Carter were slipping. They might never be dominating players again. And Dwight Gooden wasn't quite the nearly unbeatable force he had been back in 1985. So 1989 was looked upon as an important test for the entire ball club.

Even in the spring, however, there was uncharacteristic bickering. Gooden had signed a three-year, $6.7 million contract before the season started and Darryl Strawberry was already talking about having his pact extended. The popular Wally Backman was traded to open second base up for phenom Gregg Jefferies, and this move was looked upon with skepticism by some of the veterans. Backman was considered a spark plug, an igniter. Jefferies was still an unknown quantity despite his obvious potential.

There were also several spring training incidents that ended up with punches almost thrown. Plus both Mookie Wilson and Lenny Dykstra let it be known that they were tired of the centerfield platoon. They hoped Davey Johnson would go with one of them and trade the other. So it soon became obvious that the Mets were no longer one big happy family.

And when the season started it was apparent the club wasn't an awesome force on the field. The pitching was spotty as was the hitting. Strawberry was playing as if he were in a funk and both Carter and Hernandez were suddenly looking like old ball players. Young Jefferies was not only unsteady at second, but was slumping horribly at the plate. Manager Johnson stayed with him and some other players began to grouse that the youngster was receiving preferential treatment.

It wasn't long before things began going from bad to worse. In June the club finally made a move, sending Dykstra and reliever Roger McDowell to Philadelphia for Juan Samuel. Samuel was a former all-star second sacker whom the Mets decided to use in centerfield. The experiment didn't work. Samuel had problems in the field and didn't hit up to his potential.

Opposite: *Righty Ron Darling was a consistent winner for the Mets from the middle to late 1980s.*

Below: *Darryl Strawberry had an off year in 1989, batting .225 as compared to .269 in 1988.*

Above: *Doc Gooden and Gary Carter were a winning combination many times during the Mets' great years in the middle to late 1980s. When Carter left the team after the 1989 season it signaled the end of an era.*

Opposite left: *When given the opportunity to play on a regular basis, Dave Magadan came through. He batted .328 – just 7 points behind the league's best hitter.*

In another late-season move, the club dealt longtime popular Met Mookie Wilson to Toronto. So after starting the season with two centerfielders, the team now had none. It was that kind of year. When it ended, the Mets were second to the Cubs with an 87-75 record, finishing six games back. It wasn't bad, but not good enough for a team that was supposed to win easily. A look at the numbers quickly showed why.

Gooden's season, of course, ended early. Sid Fernandez emerged as the ace of the staff with a 14-5 record. Cone was 14-8, Darling 14-14, Ojeda 13-11. Myers had 24 saves, but after that the bullpen was spotty. So while the pitching was still good, it wasn't overwhelming.

The hitting didn't help either. Strawberry slumped to a .225 season with 29 homers, but just 77 RBIs. Howard Johnson had the best season with a .287 average leading to 36 homers and 101 ribbies. McReynolds was consistent with 22 homers and 85 RBIs. But Hernandez batted just .233 with 4 homers and 19 RBIs in 75 games, and Carter had an anemic .183 average with 2 homers and 15 ribbies in just 50 games. Both vets were hurt often and their futures were in doubt.

Jefferies rebounded somewhat to finish with a .258 average including 12 homers and 56 RBIs. He definitely had a future, but his presence caused a lot of problems in 1989. Newcomer Samuel batted just .235 with 11 homers and 48 RBIs. The Mets expected much more. Young players such as Mark Carreon, Mackey Sasser, Barry Lyons, and Dave Magadan all showed flashes, but didn't play enough to prove they could do it over an entire season.

So the Mets were suddenly a team in transition. They showed that just two days after the season ended when the ball club announced it would not be offering new contracts to either Gary Carter or Keith Hernandez. These were the two players generally credited with completing the transformation of the team into a winner back in 1984 and 1985. Now they were gone, free to move on. And in a way, their departure signified the end of yet another era.

It was no secret that the Mets and Davey Johnson were both on the hot seat at the outset of the 1990 season. With Frank Viola in New York for the entire year and closer John Franco coming over from Cincinnati for Randy Myers, the ball club once again was considered to have the finest pitching in the league. Juan Samuel was gone, traded to the Dodgers for first sacker Mike Marshall, a good power hitter. With Strawberry, McReynolds, Johnson, Jefferies and now Marshall, there should be plenty of power. In other words, it was time for the

Despite everything, the team stayed in the race. Then on June 19, Dwight Gooden won his 9th game of the year and 100th of his career. He was the third youngest pitcher to get 100 victories and with a 9-2 mark seemed on the way to another 20-win season. But soon after, the Doctor felt a twinge in his right shoulder. It was diagnosed as a muscle strain, but would effectively keep Gooden on the shelf the rest of the year. He would finish the season with a 9-4 mark.

Maybe the team panicked a bit after that. By August 7, the club's record was 58-51, not nearly what it was supposed to be. Chicago and Montreal were tied for first, with the Mets and Cards just four games out. So four teams were still in it and perhaps the Mets felt they had to make a move. When they did, it was a major one.

They acquired lefty pitcher Frank Viola from the Minnesota Twins in return righthander Rick Aguilera and three minor league pitchers. Some felt the team was mortgaging its future to try to win now. But Viola was considered a superstar, the American League Cy Young Award winner in 1988 with a 24-7 record. But he, too, was struggling with an 8-12 mark in 1989, so the Mets were hoping he could regain his Cy Young form.

Viola would go just 5-5 for the Mets (though he pitched better than his record showed), but the team just didn't have what it takes to win it. Strawberry and Jefferies still weren't hitting, Hernandez was hurt, and Carter's bat seemed to develop a hole in it. By September, it became apparent there would be no surge, no push to the title.

Mets to win again.

But it didn't turn out that way. After 42 games, the Mets were under .500 and struggling at 20-22. The manager got the blame and Davey Johnson was replaced in early June by former player and coach Bud Harrelson. The ball club did get back in the race and make a run at it during the second half. In fact, they actually were in first place on a few occasions, but they were brief stays. The Pittsburgh Pirates wound up capturing the National League East with the Mets 4 games behind at 91-71.

There were some fine individual performances. Viola won 20 games, while Gooden took 19 (including a great second half).

John Franco led the league in saves and Dave Magadan, taking over at first for the injured, then traded, Mike Marshall, batted .328 to come within 7 points of the batting title. Strawberry set a club record for RBIs with 108 and laced out 37 homers. But he has now signed with the Dodgers.

In addition, there were some disappointments and it is generally acknowledged that changes will have to be made before 1991. But the Mets won more than 90 games in 1990; the sixth time in seven seasons and are acknowledged as a talented team still capable of winning its division. With just a little fine tuning, the ball club should be right back in the race once again.

Above: *It was another major deal for the Mets when the team acquired former Cy Young Award winner Frank Viola from the Twins in 1989. In 1990 Viola became one of the top southpaws in the National League.*

Met Achievements

YEAR-BY-YEAR MET STANDINGS

Year	Pos.	Record	Games Behind	Manager
1962	10	40-120	60½	Stengel
1963	10	51-111	48½	Stengel
1964	10	53-109	40	Stengel
1965	10	50-112	47	Stengel/Westrum
1966	9	66-95	28½	Westrum
1967	10	61-101	40½	Westrum/Parker
1968	9	73-89	24	Hodges
1969	1	100-62	+ 8	Hodges
1970	3	83-79	6	Hodges
1971	3(T)	83-79	14	Hodges
1972	3	83-73	13½	Berra
1973	1	82-79	+ 1½	Berra
1974	5	71-91	17	Berra
1975	3(T)	82-80	10½	Berra/McMillan
1976	3	86-76	15	Frazier
1977	6	64-98	37	Frazier/Torre
1978	6	66-96	24	Torre
1979	6	63-99	35	Torre
1980	5	67-95	24	Torre
1981	5	41-62	18½	Torre
1982	6	65-97	27	Bamberger
1983	6	68-94	22	Bamberger/Howard
1984	2	90-72	6½	Johnson
1985	2	98-64	3	Johnson
1986	1	108-54	+21½	Johnson
1987	2	92-70	3	Johnson
1988	1	100-60	+15	Johnson
1989	2	87-75	6	Johnson
1990	2	91-71	4	Johnson/Harrelson

ALL-TIME MET CAREER BATTING LEADERS

Games Played	Ed Kranepool	1853
At Bats	Ed Kranepool	5436
Hits	Ed Kranepool	1418
Batting Average	Keith Hernandez	.298
Home Runs	Darryl Strawberry	215
Runs Scored	Mookie Wilson	592
Runs Batted in	Darryl Strawberry	627
Total Bases	Ed Kranepool	2047
Doubles	Ed Kranepool	225
Triples	Mookie Wilson	62

ALL-TIME MET CAREER PITCHING LEADERS

Innings Pitched	Tom Seaver	3045
Wins	Tom Seaver	198
Losses	Jerry Koosman	137
Starts	Tom Seaver	395
Games	Tom Seaver	401
Complete Games	Tom Seaver	171
Strikeouts	Tom Seaver	2541
Walks	Tom Seaver	847
Shutouts	Tom Seaver	44
Saves	Jesse Orosco	107
Earned Run Average	Tom Seaver	2.57

SINGLE-SEASON MET BATTING RECORDS

Batting Average	Cleon Jones	.340	1969
Hits	Felix Millan	191	1975
Home Runs	Darryl Strawberry	39	1987
	Darryl Strawberry	39	1988
Runs Batted In	Darryl Strawberry	108	1990
At Bats	Felix Millan	676	1975
Doubles	Howard Johnson	41	1989
Triples	Mookie Wilson	10	1984
Total Bases	Howard Johnson	319	1989
Extra Base Hits	Howard Johnson	80	1989
Walks	Darryl Strawberry	97	1987
	Keith Hernandez	97	1984
Slugging Pct.	Darryl Strawberry	.583	1987

SINGLE-SEASON MET PITCHING RECORDS

Games	Roger McDowell	75	1986
Starts	Jack Fisher	36	1965
	Tom Seaver	36	1970
	Tom Seaver	36	1973
	Tom Seaver	36	1975
Complete Games	Tom Seaver	21	1971
Wins	Tom Seaver	25	1969
Losses	Roger Craig	24	1962
	Jack Fisher	24	1965
Innings Pitched	Tom Seaver	291	1970
Strikeouts	Tom Seaver	289	1971
Walks	Nolan Ryan	116	1971
Shutouts	Dwight Gooden	8	1985
Saves	John Franco	33	1990
Earned Run Average	Dwight Gooden	1.53	1985

METS POST-SEASON RECORD

Playoffs

Year	Opponent	Win-Loss
1969	Atlanta	3-0
1973	Cincinnati	3-2
1986	Houston	4-2
1988	Los Angeles	3-4

World Series

Year	Opponent	
1969	Baltimore	4-1
1973	Oakland	3-4
1986	Boston	4-3

Left: *The Mets are treated to a tickertape parade up Broadway after winning the 1969 World Series.*

MET AWARD WINNERS

National League Cy Young Award

1969	Tom Seaver
1973	Tom Seaver
1975	Tom Seaver
1985	Dwight Gooden

National League Rookie of the Year

1967	Tom Seaver
1972	Jon Matlack
1983	Darryl Strawberry
1984	Dwight Gooden

Rawlings National League Gold Glove Winners

1970	Tommie Agee, OF
1971	Bud Harrelson, SS
1980	Doug Flynn, 2B
1983	Keith Hernandez, 1B
1984	Keith Hernandez, 1B
1985	Keith Hernandez, 1B
1986	Keith Hernandez, 1B
1987	Keith Hernandez, 1B
1988	Keith Hernandez, 1B

Index

Numbers in *italics* indicate illustrations